LS

North Norfolk saltmarshes

A
NATURE
JOURNAL

Staverton Thicks, Suffolk

A
NATURE
JOURNAL

RICHARD MABEY

Illustrations by Clare Roberts

Chatto & Windus
LONDON

Published in 1991 by
Chatto & Windus Ltd
20 Vauxhall Bridge Road
London SW1V 2SA

A CIP catalogue record for
this book is available from
the British Library.

ISBN 0 7011 3507 7

Photoset by
Rowland Phototypesetting Ltd
Bury St Edmunds, Suffolk
Printed in Great Britain by
Butler and Tanner Ltd
Frome, Somerset

To David and Janet Cobham
and to Gill,
who helped keep
the martin watch

The Pop Process
Food for Free
The Unofficial Countryside
Street Flowers
The Common Ground
The Flowering of Britain (with Tony Evans)
In a Green Shade
Cold Comforts
Oak and Company
The Frampton Flora
Gilbert White
Home Country

CONTENTS

Introduction	1
Acknowledgements	5
January	7
February	16
March	31
April	42
May	51
June	66
July	79
August	94
September	105
October	118
November	127
December	135
Epilogue	143
Index	144

INTRODUCTION

This book is a selection of entries from my natural history journals, and thus a record of the past. But it is also a kind of calendar or almanac. Unlike other kinds of diary, those that chart the natural world's annual progress all have an element of forecasting about them. The small celebrations of flowering and song, the fine days and farewells, will, barring some catastrophe, be repeated the following year. One of the things we value nature for is this sense of reassurance. 'It is,' John Fowles once wrote, 'the timelessness woven through time . . . the poetry of survival . . . Nobody who has comprehended this can feel alone in nature, can ever feel the absolute hostility of time.'

I was well into my twenties before I started writing a nature journal. But, as far back as I can remember, I was fascinated by the aura of *occasion*, by the when and where of things. I had private retreats, in woods and thickets, for particular times of day and particular moments of the year. I was hypersensitive to the emotion of seasonal ceremonies, even the catchpenny versions that marked out the school year. I yearned for leaves to break and frogs to spawn, and was happiest of all when I saw these things in one of my secret places.

In my teenage years, migrant birds were the most powerful calendar totems. But they, too, had to join moment and place together. My first swift had to be seen over a certain wood on the first day of May, the first chiffchaffs heard in the bluebell wood at the top of our road. I was as territorially devoted as a migrant bird myself, ritually treading out routes that were detailed down to the last bush.

The obsessive edge to all this faded as childhood slipped away. But not the sheer pleasure of seasonal rites, nor a growing conviction that we probably need these ways of easing age and transience just as much as our more naturally-rooted ancestors did. I still don't feel the spring is here until I have watched the first swift-race round the town; or feel I can say goodbye to the summer until I have had a meal out of doors in a Greek restaurant in London.

These are personal rites. But tokens of place and season are social symbols, too. Some – the first swallow, the last rose – are almost universal. Some are more local. My own little group of long-time friends from home has evolved its own traditions over the years – trips to Oxford at bulb time in February and punting time in summer; to Norfolk for New Year and for the samphire in August. Our annual high-spot, a kind of spring-welcoming, is the Easter Monday Morris dances in one of the Chiltern villages. Friends, not seen for years, mysteriously home in on the spot. Morris sides from the Midlands, in fantastic floral outfits, dance intense and furious shifts. For a whole day bad humour and hangovers are banished – and, almost as miraculously, the first swallows nearly always coast in over the Green Men and thwacking sticks – even in the teeth of April blizzards.

These makeshift seasonal rituals, spiced often with a very un-adult boisterousness, no doubt have a lot to do with stemming the advance of the years. But it would be pleasing to think that they also celebrated the natural virtue of renewal.

The balance between stability and change is surely at the

heart of nature's appeal to us. Its deep, predictable annual rhythms are full of subtle surprises and improvisations. Its so-called 'timelessness', as John Fowles points out, positively bristles with time, responding to light, weather and season, incorporating history and experience.

We have our seasonal bristles, too, and, in looking at nature, still see moments of promise and the facts of continuity, and a multitude of ancient, social and personal references — all of which serve to remind us that we are creatures built around biological clocks and calendars ourselves. Our natural rites don't make the world go round, but they do acknowledge that it does.

The entries in this book are chosen chiefly out of some twenty years of diary entries which record these special seasonal moments. They have been assembled as if they were an account of a single year — which, at a pinch, they could have been. But where an event is plainly a one-off (the visitation of a rare bird, for example) I have given the year. Some favourite places and activities — Oxford, watching from trains, the north Norfolk coast, exploring woods, keeping the long summer watch over nesting house martins — crop up several times throughout the year. Normally, the location where the observation is made is given, except where it is from my home patch in the north-west Chilterns. References to 'my wood' refer to Hardings Wood in Wigginton parish, an old Chiltern wood owned by me, but looked after and used by the local people.

There are two categories of entry which recur each month: a flower or plant of the month, and an introductory note on an activity (for example, listening to bird-song, seasiding in winter) that seems special for that month.

ACKNOWLEDGEMENTS

Although many of the entries here are in the form in which they were first jotted down, others have been elaborated into short essays or articles. I am grateful to the editors of the newspapers and magazines involved (*The Sunday Times*, *The Independent*, *The Sunday Telegraph* and the *Countryman*) for giving me the opportunity to pursue my seasonal preoccupations. And I owe a special vote of thanks to Roz Kidman Cox, editor of *BBC Wildlife* magazine, who, since 1988, has given me space for a personal monthly column, much of which is taken up with reflections on place and season.

My thanks also to Carmen Callil for suggesting the book, to Alison Samuel for her wise and scrupulous comments on an early draft, and to Rupert Lancaster, Richard Simon and David Cobham for their valuable comments on the text.

JANUARY

Oystercatchers, North Norfolk

NEW YEAR'S DAY *The East Anglian Coast*

When I was in my twenties I used regularly to flee to the north Norfolk or the Suffolk coast for the New Year with a group of old friends, all of us looking for an antidote to the interminable languor of a Home Counties Christmas.

The coastal landscape was incomparable in winter. The saltmarshes glittered with frost and the immense skies above were etched with the flights of wildfowl and waders. It seemed to be the best of all possible worlds: a landscape pared down to its purest essentials, yet pumped back with life by the sea.

The place has barely changed at all, but I find I look back at those Norfolk winters with an odd mixture of nostalgia and guilt. I miss the sense of freedom they represented, and the clear, *compact* winters that we seemed to be blessed with in the 1960s and early 1970s. What I am less comfortable recalling is the view I held of birds (and maybe nature as a whole) during those days spent gazing rapturously over the incoming tide. They seemed not so much living creatures as mere ornaments – props in the immense scenic drama that was played out twice daily along the coast. My diary notes are as detached as a landscape painter's: 'Whitefronts calling invisibly through the sea-fog'; 'Nine Bewick's swans strung out against the sky like a Chinese print'; 'short-eared owls and hen harriers wheeling against a great crimson sunset'.

These were, in many senses, privileged views – the product of youth, romantic optimism, and the visitor's freedom to come and go. But I am thinner-skinned now, and can't ignore the other, harsher face of winter. There is some justice in the fact that it was in north Norfolk that the change began, during a spell of severe weather early in 1978.

I was staying with friends near Burnham Market, about three miles from the coast, when the year's second bout of snowfalls began. There was a blizzard over the North Sea, followed by a dense mist that produced something close to a white-out. The next day, the shore around Holkham was littered with dying redwings which had been flying south to try to escape the worst of the freezing weather and had been caught in the fog or blizzard. They were in a pitiable and helpless state, emaciated, unable to fly, and staying hunched and motionless however close we came. A terrible darkness was spreading across their plumage, and already they seemed like mere smudges in the snow, holes where something had once been.

That day was a salutary and humbling experience, and a reminder that, however much humans share in the seasonal round and glimpse its ancient biological force, we can never completely share another creature's experience.

JANUARY 6 *North Chilterns*

A steel-grey sparrowhawk jinks down a lane just in front of my car, wings held out sharp and stiff, like a small falcon. It holds this position for more than fifty yards before sheering off over the bank, and floating over the hedge with more rounded wings. Was it hoping my car would flush out small birds?

JANUARY 16

Smart scarecrows going up in echelons in the fields.

The change in the fortunes of these ancient vernacular sculptures seemed to begin during the hard winter of 1986. Ravenous pigeons were streaming into this country from the frozen mainland of Europe, and in many rape fields the flocks were so vast that farmers responded in kind with battalions of scarers. In some places there were as many as half a dozen to a field. But they weren't ordinary Worzel Gummidges, thrown together from rags and straws. They were done up in denim jackets and M & S shirts, topped off with chicly-tied scarves. They wore fashionable pastel shades and were arranged with the casual elegance of menswear window dummies. Some even sported sunglasses. The age of the Designer Scarecrow had arrived.

Since then they have spread all over arable England. On hard-pressed farms in the Midlands, I have seen gothic scarecrows, made entirely from black and white polythene bags draped over wooden crosses, with the plastic slashed so that their limbs seem to stream out in the wind. On a Bucks smallholding I have spotted a model of a plump, black cat dangling over the vegetables. And around one of our local Big Houses, the owner has taken to putting out plywood pheasant-potters, painted bright red and yellow and holding their guns in the 'take-aim' position. In the distance they look like Rupert Bears, and the pigeons seem to find them irresistibly charming.

Like all the best grassroots fashion, the fad for new scarecrows has spawned enterprising commercial imitations. In Dorset a craftswoman has begun making miniature scarecrows as souvenirs and holiday-cottage ornaments. (Some are small enough to go in window boxes and are modelled on village elders, which must raise a few local eyebrows.)

The most striking off-shoot on the farm has been Scarey Man, a large, inflatable doll whose face has an unnerving resemblance to an Identikit villain in a stocking mask. Driven by a twelve-volt battery, Scarey Man inflates and falls over five times every twenty minutes, to accompanying siren sound effects, like a stage fight being endlessly re-hearsed in the field.

What will sociologists make of it all? A response to agriculture's worsening public image, a bit of defiant waving from the surplus lakes? Have Style Wars reached the farm at last? Or is it just the latest version of that streak in rural humour which once created irreverent misericords and rude topiary, and now adds extra flourishes to corn circles?

JANUARY 25

A kingfisher flying high over the canal with a large fish in its bill. It hits a gust of wind and stalls, and looks momentarily as ponderous as a sparrow.

JANUARY 29

Clouds of gnats dance above the lawn in the late afternoon, and a grey wagtail up from the canal flits after them, its chrome yellow underparts and steel-grey wings making an odd and cheering display of exotic colour in the winter gloom.

JANUARY, THE LAST WEEK *Severn Estuary (1)*

Flocks of teal and wigeon feeding in flooded meadows and pub gardens hundreds of yards from the river's edge.

In winter the estuarine reaches of the Severn make it stand out from all other English rivers. It is dramatic, unpredictable, rumbustious, as far from a willow-lined brook as you can imagine. It is an *epic* river, taking in two nations, half the West Country and hundreds of square miles of hectic water.

When I was at school, and drawing the outline of Britain was a regular chore, we were told to imagine the Severn as the nation's mouth. Looking at a map now, this seems more than just a useful jog to the memory. The estuary is an immense gullet, already twelve miles wide at its notional entrance between Nash and Harlestone Points. By rights it ought to have become the national maw, luring in every adventurous colonist and trader, and shifting our centre of economic gravity decisively to the west. What prevented this was the Severn mud, which is as mobile and temperamental as its water. At low tide the river shrinks to a quarter of its full width, and the estuary becomes an outsize creek, complete with a sinister fretwork of dark rock shoals and sand spits.

11

During spring tides, when the water slaps up close to the rim of the flood defence banks, it can swing to the opposite extreme. The famous Severn Bore can be stupendous at this time of year, and the wall of tidal water, created by the river's sharply funnelled profile, can charge upstream furiously enough for surfers to ride it all the way from Newnham to Gloucester.

The Severn is classic borderland, and fishing and farming have always been close partners. Salmon run a gauntlet of wicker traps that are probably prehistoric in design; elvers – the young eels that migrate in astronomical numbers up the river in early spring – are caught and eaten in the Severnside villages. Cattle still follow medieval green lanes down to grasslands that owe much of their luxuriance to past silting and flooding. But the estuary isn't as amphibious as, say, East Anglia, where much of the territory is an unresolved no-man's-land between earth and water. By the Severn, quite unequivocally, there is the river and there is the land; and the plough ridges which stretch right up to the massive sea defences show that things have gone about as far as they can in the business of turning one into the other.

This motif, of cultivated landscapes cheek by jowl with wild water, is repeated with local variations all the way along the upper reaches of the estuary. To reach Awre, the very first settlement on the north bank, you must burrow down through a network of hollow lanes with a ferny, almost Cornish luxuriance. The village itself is a cluster of houses around a soaring riverside church, and was the starting point for a ferry that used to carry charcoal from the Forest of Dean over to the village of Frampton. At Aust, in January, you can sit under the flickering shadows of the evening rush hour on the Severn Bridge and watch the dunlin flocks (the estuary holds fifty thousand of this species – nearly a fortieth of the world's population) on their downstream flight to roost.

Between these two villages is a landscape of fields and orchards and straggling hedges full of pollard ashes. It is one of the few places where pollards are still regularly cut for firewood, each tree once every ten years or so, and the pale ends of freshly-lopped and stacked branches gleam behind the bare hedges. Amidst these pastoral prospects you catch bizarre glimpses of the estuary's other human landscapes. A dip in the road, and the high-tech docks at Sharpness rear up momentarily between two barns. Oldbury nuclear power station is framed by garlands of pear-tree mistletoe.

And as you drive south from the Severn Bridge, the skyline begins to fill with cooling towers and gasholders, wreathed in pale orange smoke. This is Avonmouth, a chemical metropolis that covers close on ten square miles and whose effluent comprises one of the most concentrated mixtures of pollutants of any British estuary.

Yet, one January, I was panning my binoculars away from one of the big chemical company's discharge pipes onto the tussocky waste ground that lies between Avonmouth and the river, when a patch of brown detritus appeared to lift clear of the ground and float towards me. It was a short-eared owl, its huge tiger-yellow eyes glaring full ahead. It turned off when it was about ten yards away, and I watched it circle over Severn Beach's caravan site, past the pub garden and the new holiday flats development, its plumage a chequer of buff and chestnut in the evening sun.

These odd conjunctions are typical of Severnside and continue even at the Wildfowl Trust's famous reserve at Slimbridge. The shallow bay between Slimbridge village and the river is one of the last patches of real marshland on the estuary, and was a haven for waterbirds long before Peter Scott first rented it in 1946. Now it is probably the most civilised bird observatory in the world. There are hides sponsored by banks and binocular firms, admonitory and educational hides ('Remember, geese have ears!') double-storeyed, picture-windowed and centrally-heated hides. From them you can gaze out over a teeming landscape in which it can be difficult to separate the wild and the tame. Throughout the winter swarms of geese mill about in the lakes, the pinioned exotics tempting in the wild migrants. Bewick's swans commute between the wet meadows and the feeding pens. And on the edge of the reserve, knot and dunlin flocks swirl about like a denser kind of smoke in front of the plumes rising from the Welsh factories over the river.

FLOWER OF THE MONTH

In mild winters there are always flowers about early in the New Year. Many have probably never been out of bloom. Fast-growing annual weeds, such as groundsel and white and red dead-nettles, flower all the year in open ground. So does hairy bittercress, a small but shapely member of the cabbage family, whose tiny four-petalled flowers are carried above a loose rosette of leaves. Bittercress's tolerance of winter weather is helped by its extraordinary ability to scatter seeds around. The finger-shaped pods form soon after flowering, and as they ripen so their tissues dry and tighten until they are like stretched elastic. Eventually they reach such a pitch of tension that even a gust of wind can cause the pod to split violently lengthways. The casing curls back, banana-skin style, and the twenty or so seeds are thrown off, sometimes as far as a yard away.

There may be perennials in bloom, too, especially grass-land flowers that have been encouraged to put on new growth during the winter by late-autumn mowing. The odd daisy and dandelion opens on lawns if there is enough sun. Hogweed umbels form a few inches above the ground on roadside verges. Even primroses may put out the odd tentative flower, though they will be half-shut, pursed, until the warm weather sets in.

Hairy bittercress

But the earliest flower of the year, the first true precursor of the woodland spring, is the spurge laurel, one of our two native Daphnes. From mid-January sometimes, this evergreen shrub carries spikes of modest yellowish flowers above its glossy, holly-green leaves. They have, like many other early flowers, a faint but teasingly musky scent, a lure for any insects that might be tempted out by unseasonal warmth. But the flowers will open even in the frosts, and, for anyone who takes the trouble to sniff, are a cheering reminder that not all the chemistry of spring is dependent on good weather.

Spurge laurel occurs in open woodland in central and southern England, thinning out in the north. In parts of the New Forest it grows on quite acid soils, but chiefly it is a plant of the chalk, and the Chilterns is the place to see it at its best, under a tangle of old man's beard at the edge of a wood, or in dark drifts against the pale trunks of the beeches.

15

FEBRUARY

Oxford Ragwort growing on a wall, Oxford.

Trees in bud and the blooming of the first woodland flowers make February a good time to begin exploring old woods again – what one might call 'woodcrawling'. Britain has some three hundred thousand hectares of 'ancient' wood-land, and like parish churches they are rich in physical evidence of their past.

But the term 'ancient woodland' needs some explanation, since it doesn't mean simply woodland containing old trees. It normally refers to sites which have been continuously wooded since 1600. This date marks the watershed between two separate traditions of managing woodlands: forestry, with its artificially created plantations, often of exotic species; and the older tradition of woodmanship, which relied on the continuous cropping and regrowth of naturally-occurring native trees. Part of the fascination of pre-1600, naturally-sprung woods is that they are likely to have – almost by definition – more natural features than artificially created plantations. There is even a chance that they are growing on sites which have been continuously wooded since the end of the last Ice Age, and so may have biological links with the primeval wildwood which cloaked most dry land ten thousand years ago.

Yet the reason they have survived is usually because they have had some kind of useful social role. This is not what the popular mythology of the English greenwood maintains. Most of us were brought up on this version of woodland history, and told how the land was once covered with an immense oak forest. This survived the onslaughts of the early settlers, to be almost wiped out by the plunderings of the iron industry and the need to maintain the British fleet. The national woodland estate was only saved from total obliteration by the far-sighted plantings of the eighteenth- and nineteenth-century landowners. In short, the legend teaches us that felling and using trees destroys woodland, and that deliberate tree planting is necessary to restore them.

It is a sympathetic myth, but differs from the real history in almost every particular. The primeval wildwood, for example, was a constantly varying tapestry of a score of different tree species. In the south of England, the now scarce small-leaved lime was as common as oak. Clearance for crop-growing and settlement was under way very early, more than six thousand years ago on current estimates. As the area of woodland declined, what remained was used with increasing ingenuity and care.

By the time of the Domesday Survey of 1086 less than a fifth of the original forest cover remained, and was being managed as a mosaic of wastes, hunting chases, wooded

Coppiced woodland, Suffolk.

areas where cattle grazed, and enclosed coppices where fuelwood and building timber grew. There were few planta-tions until the very end of the seventeenth century, yet the productivity of the nation's woods was remarkably high. By 1600, when the trade in the coal and cheap Scandinavian softwoods was still comparatively small, Britain's population of some seven million was more or less self-sufficient in timber and fuel from a total area of tree-land rather less than we have at present. One eminent woodland historian has called wood 'the North Sea gas of pre-1800 England'. That these ancient woods were able to go on producing a seemingly inexhaustible supply of fuel and timber is due to the simple but persistently ignored fact that our native broadleaf trees are capable of regenerating from the stump when felled or lopped, and of doing so indefinitely.

You do not need to take this alternative woodland history on trust. It is all there, preserved in the intricate structure of the woods themselves. Here and there, on inland cliffs, unstable shorelines and other habitats too precarious or inaccessible to have been worked, you can see something of the variety of the original wildwood. On upland scree slopes, for example, there may be patches of juniper, birch and aspen which are probably much like the shrubby woodland which pioneered the reafforestation of Britain after the retreat of the glaciers. Diminutive ash-woods, pruned by wind and grazing animals, shelter in the cracks of upland limestone 'pavements', especially in the Yorkshire Dales.

But the majority of surviving ancient woods have been worked in some ways, from the alder dingles on the Welsh borders, once cut for clogs, to the great West Country oakwoods whose bark was used in the tanning trade. Both these were managed by the practice known as 'coppicing', in which the top growth of the trees was cut back to the base every ten or fifteen years. Also coppiced were the gorge

19

woods that run along the banks of the River Wye, and which contain almost our entire range of native trees and shrubs. They were harvested largely to supply the local iron smelting works with fuel. It is no coincidence that many of the most densely and continuously wooded areas of Britain – the Weald, the Forests of Dean in Gloucestershire, Wyre in Worcestershire and Furness in Lancashire, for instance – occur precisely where there were flourishing iron mining and smelting industries. The ironworks needed a continuing supply of wood charcoal, and the owners made sure that the woods which produced it were well looked after.

Various kinds of usefulness ensured the conservation of other areas of woodland. The Chilterns, for example, were a major source of firewood for London until the advent of cheap coal. In the nineteenth century they found a new role when many of the old mixed coppices were converted into beech 'high forest' to provide timber for the chair-makers of High Wycombe.

Beyond the coppices there is the legacy of a quite separate tradition, so-called 'wood-pasture', in which the growing of wood is combined with the raising of cattle or deer. In this tradition are medieval deer parks, like Moccas in Herefordshire and Bradgate in Leicestershire, and the many wooded commons of southern England – Burnham Beeches, Epping, the New Forest, the Mens in Sussex. In all these places firewood was lopped above the level at which cattle browsed, by the process known as 'pollarding'.

But it isn't just the big woods that have preserved a record of how they were used. History is inscribed – ingrained, so to speak – in the smallest parish woods.

Much can be read from the form of individual trees. Rings of small trunks or poles, apparently springing from a single base, are known as *stools*, and are the form in which trees grow when coppiced regularly. When one of these poles is cut, counting its rings will tell you not how old the tree is but when it was last cropped. There may also be *giant stools*, many yards across, which have come to look like a group of separate trees, because the centre of the stool has rotted away. Some are probably over a thousand years old and may have been coppiced fifty times in their long lives. *Pollards* bear sheaves of branches beginning about eight to ten feet above ground, often on immensely broad and gnarled trunks, especially of oak and beech. *Maidens*, or standards, are uncut trees deliberately encouraged to grow tall and straight to provide better quality timber for building or furniture. They are most usually found in plantations, but were also grown amongst coppice-wood.

Sometimes you may see a short pollard or *stub*, with a trunk about three or four feet tall. These are just one of a large range of features originally employed to mark bound-aries around, or inside, woods. The commonest of these is the *bank and ditch*. Ancient woodbanks are usually massive and sinuous. Since one of their original functions was to keep grazing animals (both wild and domesticated) away from the young shoots of growing coppice, their accom-panying ditch was usually on the outside. A reverse bank, with the ditch on the *inside*, is typical of wooded deer parks and commons, where the intention was to keep the animals in. Some woodbanks still carry the remains of hedges that were often grown on top of them (though wooden fences were used as well). And there are some woods in the Wye Valley where the boundaries and internal compartments are marked by stone walls.

In addition there is the wildlife, which is also a feature of ancient woods. Dormice prefer long-established woods. So do some of our more glamorous butterflies, such as the white admiral and the purple emperor. Most striking are their special flowers, usually known as 'ancient woodland indicators'. There are something like a hundred species of wild flower and shrub more or less confined to anciently wooded sites because of their poor colonising ability, including such favourites as wood sorrel, wood anemone, sweet woodruff and early purple orchid. There are also lichens and beetles associated with the old trees and dead wood of ancient wood pastures, and mosses confined to the damp habitats of long-established woods near the Atlantic coast, such as the Lake District oakwoods.

There are many other areas with a good variety of ancient woods apart from those mentioned above, including: Cornwall (estuarine and coastal woods, see p. 40); Hampshire (New Forest, beech 'hangers' etc); Cotswolds (beechwoods rich in orchids and lilies); Lincolnshire (ancient limewoods); Suffolk and Essex (large numbers of small, worked coppices).

FEBRUARY 2 CANDLEMAS

The traditional date for snowdrops. The pure white flowers were put in bunches in the windows of monasteries and abbeys to commemorate this feast of the Purification of the Virgin.

FEBRUARY, THE SECOND WEEK *Oxford*

The centre of the city turned into a miniature Venice by flash floods. Mallards cannot swim against the spate in the Cherwell. Magdalen Meadows have become a lake, and snowdrops are flowering underwater, waving in slow motion every time the wind ruffles the surface.

Oxford, city of greening spires, is full of seasonal echoes, and has been a favourite retreat of mine since student days. This is partly due to the comings-and-goings associated with the university year, which add a kind of tidal cycle to the ordinary annual round. But there are relics of earlier seasonal rites, too, not least in one of the most fascinating and lively floras of any English city. Oxford is awash with plants. Herbs from monastic cloisters survive on old walls and in cracks in the pavement. The college gardens are full of plants and trees donated by eighteenth-century vicars and twentieth-century globe-trotting dons. Along the back lanes and the rivers, wild and domesticated plants – alpine anemones, mistletoe, deadly nightshade – rub shoulders in a way that seems entirely in order for the home of lost causes. Oxford's own ragwort, which escaped from the arcane reaches of the Botanic Gardens to become a rampant national weed, is a classic example.

FEBRUARY 7

A grey, cool day. A flock of about fifteen siskins, wintering here from eastern Europe, hurtle into the pussy willow, quite surrounding a solitary greenfinch, which peers about in amazement at these diminutive images of himself. Then they sweep off again to the north-east.

FEBRUARY 9

Total eclipse of the moon, 1990.

I see the first stages as I am driving up to the north Norfolk coast. It begins as I am passing Thetford, at dusk, with a thin incandescent halo round the moon, as pink and thready as candy-floss. I watch the finale from North Creake. At full eclipse, the moon doesn't vanish at all, as I had expected, but becomes three-dimensional, and the dull, bleached brown of an old skull. Chastening to think it is the earth's shadow doing this.

MID-FEBRUARY (1986)

This is often the coldest time of the year, and large numbers of birds visit gardens to be fed. The 1986 freeze-up is the second most severe this century, with sub-zero temperatures persisting from February 5 until the first week of March. I all but abandon work, dashing out every few hours to restock the feeding station, and between times peering anxiously through my study window at how the garden flock is faring.

They seem to be doing rather well. But their survival is due as much to their own ingenuity and good neighbourliness as to my handouts. The deeper the frost bites, the more the entire local assemblage of birds seems to begin feeding as a community. By some not very polite peering over neighbours' fences, I can see that there is a loosely-knit feeding flock of a dozen or so species which ranges over an area of about four acres. They swirl about rather like a human crowd, or queue, concentrating very quickly once the vanguard has set down in a particular spot, and often ignoring well-stocked gardens for the sake of group security. There they stay until they are disturbed or the food supply runs out, still keeping together as they fly on to the next station.

Inside this large group there is great variety and inventiveness in patterns of feeding. A mistle thrush spends an hour picking out the orange seeds of the gladdon irises. A blackbird masters the art of hovering in order to snatch snowberries off the bush. A small flock of goldfinches shin up the dried-out stalks of a lavender bush, shredding the dried flower spikes in a cloud of chaff and flashing yellow wings. I spot another goldfinch feeding *under* the snow, where little caves have formed over dead tufts of forget-me-not. Almost every bird eats peanuts, both from nut-bags and scattered on the planks with which I have criss-crossed the lawn. I watch a blackbird alternating his nut-nibbling with sips of snow.

This year it is the siskins which dominate – and almost monopolise – the nut-bags. They are exquisite to watch,

Birds feeding in the garden

vastly more delicate feeders than the excitable tits. They hang on the bags upside down and *pick* at the nuts, as if they are using chopsticks. Not so the nuthatches, which simply yank the nuts out whole. One morning I watch a pair virtually empty a whole bag. They don't eat the nuts, but squirrel them away in cracks in the wattle fencing.

Black-headed gulls polish off stale crusts and crumpets first thing in the morning, but never stay for anything in smaller portions. Starlings dance with excitement on blocks of fat. A rather shy corn bunting quite properly nibbles corn at the edge of the swarms of more adventurous chaffinches and sparrows. One morning I watch a carrion crow, familiar with the nature of the national loaf, pick up a crust of bread, carry it to the unfrozen birdbath, and *dunk* it in the water. It stays there several minutes, repeatedly dipping the remains as it eats.

Not a single bird, I am pleased to say, behaves with the crass aggression of a blackbird I watched the previous winter. This reduced itself to a gaunt, exhausted shadow by chasing off every other blackbird that ventured into the garden, so that it had almost no time to feed itself. Our fieldfare, however, comes close.

It arrived on the fifth day of the freeze-up, a ragged, piratical creature which looked as if it had barged its way through most of the gardens in southern England to get here. It barely leaves the garden during the next three weeks, and during that time consumes more than ten pounds of Bramley apples. It is a ferocious feeder, attacking the apples with such force that it sometimes staggers over backwards from the recoil; and it will defend its territory just as vigorously. It sees off two mistle thrushes – no mean feat – in real feather-pulling brawls, and early on in its stay chases off anything remotely resembling a thrush that comes within ten feet. In the end it is forced to adopt better manners by the sheer numbers of starlings, which scrump the apples whenever it is otherwise engaged. But it remains a touchy character, given to extravagant fannings of the tail.

By judicious spacing of the planks I am eventually able to get three fieldfares feeding amicably on the lawn, but they all leave on the day of the thaw. So do the corn bunting and the yellowhammers. The nuthatches return briefly and make a few perfunctory searches for hidden nuts, and the siskins actually increase in numbers with the thaw.

All in all, I think our neighbourhood flock has come through moderately intact. I hope I am not sentimentalising the reasons for this. I don't believe that birds show conscious altruism to each other, but I find it heartening that a spirit of live-and-let-live should prevail in times of hardship, even if it is only in the interest of survival.

FEBRUARY 14 *Valentine's Day*

First blackbird's song wafting from the back of the aptly named Sanctuary health-club in Covent Garden.

Coax a celandine into flower with a sunray lamp as a Valentine gift.

FEBRUARY 21

On this day in 1978 there was the last great glazed frost, or ice storm, of recent years. It brought much of southern England to a halt, and the police prohibited all non-essential traffic movements in the West Country.

These extraordinary events, which occur when freezing rain falls onto already frozen ground, are unusual at any time, and may become more so if the trend towards mild winters continues. They can be astonishingly beautiful, seeming to coat the entire landscape in glass, but are devastating in their effects on living things. In the worst example this century, on January 27, 1940, birds were killed in mid flight when their wings froze solid, cats were iced to branches, and ponies on Plynlimon in Wales were frozen to death inside coffins of ice. On the trees leaves rattled like castanets, and telegraph wires rotated under their loads of ice (one stretch in Gloucestershire carried eleven tons between just two posts) until they were adorned with upward-pointing icicles.

FEBRUARY, LATE

Barn owls seen more often in the day time, as they begin to build up fat for the breeding season.

Early this century the 'Transactions of the Norfolk Naturalists' Society' carried an extraordinary account of a pair seen on a February afternoon, and appearing to the observer to be 'luminous'. There was a light mist in the air, and they were floating like will-o'-the-wisps over a patch of marshy ground. One 'emerged from a covert about two hundred yards distant, flying backwards and forwards across the field, at times approaching within fifty yards from where I was standing . . . it literally lit up the branches of the trees as it flew past'. The owls had probably picked up phosphorescence from roosting in the crumbling 'touchwood' of a tree affected by honey fungus, and were eerie enough to convince one astonished Norfolk naturalist that they had the power to generate their own illumination.

Barn owls are creatures of the half-light in many senses, and have always been looked on with a mixture of admiration and superstitious nervousness. Of all our birds of prey they have lived on the closest terms with human beings, and have been surrounded by mystery and mythology. The owl family's Latin name *Strix* was the Roman word for witch, and there are stories of owls being burned for witchcraft in the Middle Ages. The barn owl's screeching call was an almost universal omen of bad luck, and dead birds were nailed to barn doors to frighten off evil intruders. Yet they have a parallel, more benign image as cullers of rats and mice, bringers of luck, village familiars.

Of all the barn owls I have watched – fewer, sadly, each year – I cannot recall ever seeing one more than a few hundred yards from some kind of human settlement. They will breed not just in barns but in any kind of man-made structure – chapels, mine-shafts, even in the supports of motorway bridges. They hunt in the margins of the parish landscape, too, along the boundary hedges and green lanes and muddled streamside roughs. Their open, inquisitive faces, that seem to be mounted directly onto the wings, give them the look of guardian spirits as they patrol the bounds.

In the Cornish churchyard of St Filii de los Eglosros, one last day of winter, I saw a barn owl cross paths with a tramp headed east with a full back-pack. In Dorset, the writer Kenneth Allsop once showed me a barn owl peering inscrutably out of a hole in an old lime kiln. In East Anglia they were constant evening companions during the 1960s and early '70s, quartering the village greens or dipping along the verges in front of the car.

A barn owl looks quite weightless when it is hunting, seeming almost to be drifting over the ground. Then it will suddenly throw its wings forward, hover briefly and corkscrew down onto its invisible prey. Gilbert White described the flight perfectly: 'Owls move in a buoyant manner, as if lighter than air; they seem to want ballast'. He suspected that it was their soft and pliant plumage that enabled them to hunt so successfully while it was still daylight. 'Perhaps it may be necessary that the wings of these birds should not make much resistance or rushing, that they may be enabled to steal through the air unheard upon a nimble and watchful quarry.'

Alas, the sight of hunting barn owls is now a rare one. There are probably less than five thousand pairs surviving in England and Wales, only a fifth of the numbers in the 1930s. Busy roads, agricultural poisons, and cool, wet breeding seasons have all taken their toll. But the major factor in the decline is almost certainly the loss of those unkempt, marginal habitats that are the birds' favourite hunting ground.

Recently the uncovering of an ancient barn owl roost has

shown just how much the bird's feeding habits have been constrained in the past seventy years. The site was an old chimney stack in a house just a mile from Gilbert White's village of Selborne. When it was opened up for renovation, the owner discovered three sackfuls of owl pellets. Building records showed that the chimney had been capped since 1913, and the pellets had been protected from the weathering agents that normally break them down in open roosting sites.

What was most remarkable was the composition of the pellets, and the immense variety of food which the owls then took. Among over eight hundred identifiable prey items were fourteen different species of mammal – including water shrew, mole, Natterer's bat, weasel and dormouse. There were also fragments of frogs, insects and small birds, including swallows, yellowhammers and blackbirds. This mix is vastly richer than any that has been identified in modern barn owl pellets, and these pellets, preserved in their original site, are a kind of fossil, a reminder of the diversity of the pre-First War countryside.

FLOWER OF THE MONTH

Stinking hellebore, *Helleborus foetidus*, in the dark woods of the Hampshire Weald. The plants are stiff and shiny, as if they have been carved out of wax, and the sprays of yellow-green flowers – each edged with claret – stand out against the dark yews and hollies. The leaves do have an unpleasant smell, a little like the mousey tang of hemlock, but its name does the plant a disservice. Some local tags, such as 'bears-foot' and the cryptic 'setterwort' are more appealing.

MARCH

Black poplar

Walking in early March often has the feel of a beating of the bounds. The grass is growing on the footpaths again, the first buds breaking on the trees, and it is possible to see how the landscape has fared over the winter. I always check on some favourite personal landmarks at this time of year: a clump of green hellebore in an ice-house copse, first recorded in a Hertfordshire flora in 1849; the ancient black poplar that marks where the parish and county boundaries meet on a remote farm, and which is being slowly whittled away by gales; our precarious local oxlip colonies, which shouldn't really be growing in this part of England at all. And by the middle of the month there are returning summer birds to listen out for as well.

A mild March always stirs up the desire to tramp fresh

31

pastures, too. It is beguiling to plan these on a map, to try and plot a route that joins up tracks and lanes, and takes in an unfamiliar wood or two without going over the same ground twice. But increasingly the countryside is full of hazards that you can't anticipate in advance : guard dogs, electric fences, glass on walls, footpaths blocked by barbed wire or drenched by agricultural chemicals. Even on a public road you are not immune. One bright and blowy afternoon recently, I was driving off for an afternoon's walk with the sun-roof open for the first time in the year, when the car suddenly began to fill with fertiliser pellets, carried on the wind from a tractor scattering them in the adjacent field.

These days finding one's way round barricaded and privatised Britain needs a combination of cunning and stealth, and a willingness to breach barriers that natural justice – and the law, as often as not – insist shouldn't be there in the first place.

MARCH 8

The Bourne stream in full spate. It is our local winterbourne, one of those underground streams of the chalk country that only rise to the surface after heavy winter rains.

I'd seen it from a distance a few days before, a glinting ribbon of water snaking down from the hills. Now it is a sizeable, rushing brook that looks as old as the surrounding hills. It emerges from a seam between the clay and under-lying chalk, fed by accumulated rainwater overflowing from aquifers deep below the surface. Half a mile downstream from the source it is four feet wide and flowing as fast as I can walk. In no more than four weeks it has formed its own oxbows and torrents and eddies, and underneath them the spring grass is waving as silkily as waterweed. In one dip the winterbourne has made a pool by the edge of a wood, and bubbles rising from the buried air pockets look like summer midges settling on the surface. It feels like a good omen, and, for a few moments, I am seized by the conviction that a first precocious swallow will come coasting down the valley.

A mile further on the stream has flooded a group of low-lying pastures, and flocks of fieldfare and redwing are feeding at the edge of the water. A snipe jinks in the distance, and much closer, a heron lopes up from a pond that last carried water when I was a teenager.

These winter-flowing streams are, oddly, often taken as signs of bad luck. In Gilbert White's day their appearance was believed to presage a bad harvest. In February 1774 he wrote:

> *The landsprings, which we call lavants, break out much on the downs of Sussex, Hampshire and Wiltshire. The country people say that when lavants rise, corn will always be dear; meaning that when the earth is so glutted with water as to send forth springs on the downs and uplands, that the corn-vales must be drowned.*

And on this day, March 8, in 1774, a furious new spring caused a huge landslip in the village of Hawkley, three miles from White's Selborne.

A similar belief lingers in the Chilterns, and our winterbourne is believed to be a 'woe-water' and to flow only in times of war or dire trouble. But it has never done this in my lifetime, and has always seemed much more like harbinger and symbol of spring, and of the rising sap to come.

MARCH 10

A sunny day with temperatures above 20°C (68°F). Long-tailed tits are building in the cypress tree, and gathering spiders' webs from the guttering.

MARCH 12 *Ouse Washes, Cambridgeshire*

A raw, foggy day but thousands of wild swans and wigeon are whistling out on the marshes. Oddly stirring to be able to hear them but not see them, out in the mist on the far side of the flood-banks.

MARCH 13 *The Vale of Aylesbury*

The pollard black poplars that line the stream edges and field dykes have an amber shine against the grey skies. It is one of the most spectacular sights of spring, not visible on such a scale anywhere else in Britain. These pollards are the largest concentration of what is now our rarest timber tree, *Populus nigra* var. *betulifolia*, and this late winter glow is a kind of vegetable blush, an anticipation of spring growth. The colour begins in the young ochre twigs and ginger-shellaced buds, bleeds into the straw-yellow flower stalks and, by the end of the month, bursts into streams of voluptuous crimson catkins.

It is remarkable that such a conspicuous and magnificent tree should have passed out of common knowledge for so long. Until about twenty years ago the native black poplar was either overlooked altogether, or assumed to be just a rather odd variety of the Lombardy poplars and 'hybrid Italian blacks' so beloved of municipal authorities. Yet there

34

is really no mistaking the mature trees at any time of the year. They have massive, fissured trunks, covered with bosses and burrs, and often develop a decided lean in middle age. The branches turn down towards their ends, then sweep up again into sheaves of twigs which, once the catkins have gone, carry dense masses of shiny, beech-shaped leaves. You can often spot them from a long way off, hunched in distant fields in the Cheshire plain, or leaning solitarily in Thames-side plots.

When the tree was 're-discovered' in the 1970s, it was believed there might be only a thousand specimens left in Britain. But extensive survey work has since shown that, though undeniably scarce, it is scattered throughout England and Wales, mainly on flood plains in the lowlands. But in fifteen years of searching only one natural seedling was discovered. In the wild, black poplar seeds need to fall on mud which is still wet in June, and which remains damp and bare during the seedlings' first critical months. Conditions like this became rare once serious agricultural drainage had started in the sixteenth century. Since then almost all black poplars have been grown from deliberately planted cuttings, as boundary trees or for their timber. The whole British population is now a kind of ghost, an echo of a wilder landscape which remained obstinately full of water even in the height of summer.

MARCH 14 *Chilterns*

After a barren gap of nearly fifteen years there are elms in flower again. They are just small trees at present, but covered with tufts of crimson flowers behind which the greenish-yellow seed-discs are already forming.

Dutch elm disease seems everywhere to be in retreat, and

the suckers which survived the death of their parent trees are now escaping the disease until they are ten or more years old. Those that do eventually succumb no longer invariably die, and sometimes sprout new leaves next year, as if they had suffered nothing worse than a bout of seasonal allergy. There are even new suckers springing up around stumps which apparently had been dead for a decade.

This is much as elm experts had predicted. Some local trees have proved immune to the disease, but for the most part the remission is the result of native bacterial infections and insect predators at last attacking the dutch elm fungus, which is believed to have been brought in from Canada on imported timber.

MARCH, SECOND WEEK *The Blackdown Hills, Somerset*

March, good for walking while the weather is cool and the country lanes relatively empty, is also ideal for motoring expeditions, especially to unknown regions. The Blackdowns are a remote, hidden patch, and I once did a whistle-stop tour of them in my car, seeing if I could get my bearings and catch their essence in a single day's touring.

They lie only a few miles south of the Quantocks and south-east of Exmoor, but as you drive across the Vale of Taunton there is no doubt that you are entering a different region. Beyond Staple Fitzpaine the back lanes suddenly become feral, snaking round dog-leg bends and plunging between turf and chert-stone banks. A mile further on you meet the long road that stretches east—west along the ridge of the hills between Wellington and Ilminster, and can see that this unevenness is part of the basic structure of the place. The hills are an outcrop of Upper Greensand, which has weathered into a steep, bluff scarp along the northern edge. Down to the south the sandstone has been eroded into long finger-like ridges with deep combes and valleys between them. There are patches of woodland all along the northern ridge, ash and hazel chiefly, heavily interplanted with conifers.

But it is the beeches that stand out. They are one of the region's trademarks, and also one of its puzzles. They crowd along the road edges as tightly as plane trees do beside French roads. Most seem to be about a hundred and fifty years old, and probably date from the era of Parliamentary Enclosure, during which large areas of pasture and open field were parcelled up with new hedges. Yet the further you wander into the woodland zone, the more the beeches seem to occur on features that look vastly older than the mid-nineteenth century. Knotty, forked beeches range along the interior banks of coppice woods. Broad beech coppice stools top some of the field boundaries. At Dommett, in the south-east, there is a long tunnel of beeches along the side of what seems to be an ancient green lane, parallel with the metalled road. They are immensely tall, and their roots, swathed with moss, have grown down over the turf banks, giving them the odd look of land-bound mangroves. These Wessex beech hedges (there are similar, but less gothic rows around Exmoor and the Quantocks) are a mystery. Why such uniform planting of a tree whose leaves and shoots are a favourite with browsing cattle? Why beech at all, in a country of oaks and storm winds, which in recent years have torn many of the shallow root systems out of the ground?

It is a mild, breezy day, and I set off west, towards Hemyock. But no sooner have I struck off the ridge road, than I am lost. Blackdown's road signs are in wonderful, continental disorder – broken off, uprooted, nameless, and often turned tantalisingly half-round. Place names flash past that I can't trace on the Ordnance Survey map draped over the passenger seat. But getting lost, of course, is much the best way to discover a place. So I simply turn the car towards the most tempting direction at each junction and press on. I drop down narrow hollow-ways, whose boundary banks are studded with wall pennywort. The fleshy, round leaves are only a foot or so from the car window. Beyond the banks is a muddle of odd-shaped pastures and hazel coppices, knitted together with dense double hedges.

Then, by a tributary of the River Culm I spot the first wild daffodils. They are growing on a diminutive wooded peninsula jutting out into the stream, true, bi-coloured Lent lilies. I turn a corner and they are everywhere, covering the hedge-banks and spreading in great masses under the streamside alders where the first lambs are grazing. They are even growing round the foot of a signpost that seems, for once, to be accurate, and tells me that I am in Leigh and moving south-east towards Dunkeswell.

I meander about like this for a while, speeding through the dull enclosure landscapes on the scarps, burrowing down into the stream-cut combes. Every valley has a distinct character, but they are all modelled on a pattern of dense, intimate fieldscapes in the bottoms and ragged patches of woodland higher up the slopes.

Most of the villages are built from local chert-stone. Chert is the flint of sandstone country, pale, massy, and making the farmstead and cottages seem like extensions of the stony landscape. At Clayhidon, many of the buildings front right onto the lane. Early this century this village was a popular weekend retreat for painters of the Camden Town Group, though it isn't easy to see how their austere, geometric style could have been inspired by these profuse landscapes. The lively and eclectic music festival that used to be held at Upottery seemed more in keeping with the place.

Upottery is named after the River Otter, which in turn is

Wild daffodils, Dymock churchyard

named after the animal. Otters are scarce in the Blackdown rivers now, but the animal seems to me an apt symbol for the region. It is a thoroughly ottery landscape, full of holts and hideaways and runs, and just the place to wake up the senses at the start of spring.

March 21 Spring Equinox *The River Fal*

Woodcrawling in Cornwall. Around the estuary of the Fal, at the spring equinox, the sea creeps up through the alder and willow carr and floods the lower reaches of the oakwoods.

Tidal woods are extraordinary places, incongruous mixes of the solidity of trees and the urgent, capricious ebb and flow of the sea. They are rare places too, since woods don't often have a chance to mature in the intertidal zone.

But the Fal estuary is exceptional. The river is a natural drain for much of the heavy rain that falls on Bodmin Moor, and carries with it immense quantities of white silt washed out of the china clay beds below. It funnels through steep-sided valleys on its way to the sea, and, since the Middle Ages, has swung between silting and flooding. In the late eighteenth century silting gained the upper hand, and the woods began to spread across the floodplain.

Silting was increased in the nineteenth century by the china clay workings at St Austell, which still discharge enough sediment to turn the Fal and its tributaries the colour of clotted cream. The most truly tidal section of the wood now stretches from the bridge at Ruan Lanihorne, where the kaolin-coloured water spreads like a stain across the estuarine grasses, to Tregony, three miles inland. But most of the local creeks and low-lying corners have some trace of the ancient mix of trees and sea. West of Ruan the road cork-screws up through Lamorran Wood, fording a point where white, brackish water seeps over and under the tarmac. The sea itself lies just inside the wood, lapping a bank of Cornish elms and primroses. At St Michael Penkevil, where the Fal joins the Truro river, there is even an estuarine deer park.

After the highest equinoctial tides, the whole of this landscape – oak trunks, lichens, primrose banks, and pastures – can be covered with a thin film of white clay.

FLOWER OF THE MONTH

Prompted by the Blackdown daffodils I go to see how our local colonies are faring. They look every bit as exuberant as their West Country cousins, the floppy soft-textured flowers on their short, pert stalks, defiant in close-cropped paddocks, glimmering under hedges, ringing the winter wheat fields.

The wild daffodil is one of the more paradoxical of our wild flowers. It seems quite indestructible in its favoured spots, and still puts on a superb show in such famous sites as Grasmere in the Lakes, Farndale in Yorkshire, the Teign Valley in Devon, and the countryside round Dymock in Gloucestershire. There are small but agreeable constellations, too, in wooded Hampshire hangers, in Sussex copses and even in East Anglian churchyards.

But nationally, it must have diminished massively since the time John Gerard described it in 1597 as 'growing everywhere through England'. Yet the tide in the Lent lily's fortunes may be turning. The fashion for 'wild gardens' has resulted in it becoming a popular species in cultivation, and there are already signs that it is escaping back into the wild from these cosseted colonies.

41

APRIL

Oxlips

Birds have been singing since mid-February, but during April and May, the heart of the breeding season, the chorus becomes denser and louder as our native songsters are joined by migrant warblers from the tropics.

At this time of the year I sometimes try to draw up a list of *Desert Island* birdsongs, the sounds I could least bear to be without in spring. I also ponder why the territorial signals of one order of creation – purely functional we are told – should be so appealing to another.

As a groundbase I have tried listing those songs that I relish for their musical qualities alone. I get no further than the pure, treble voice of an early season blackcap. Every other sound is enmeshed in tangles of memory and association. There are songs which conjure up favourite places, childhood holidays, heartbreaks, adventures, the comings-and-goings of whole seasons. Even the blackbird's nonchalant warblings, so familiar and conversational as to be almost hackneyed, can make my throat catch. Whenever I hear the first of the year (cutting clear across the traffic noise in London, as often as not) I am fourteen years old again, listening to them gossip in the garden lilacs. It is a memory of a quite precise moment: the first week of the Easter holiday, the evenings drawing out, and enough light at last for a walk after tea.

Birdsongs seem especially powerful at evoking moments of the year, which in turn can seem incomplete without them. In early March there are mistle thrushes – stormcocks as they are sometimes known – skirling through the gales. In high summer, wood pigeons calling endlessly in the woods, like birds murmuring in a dream. And then the thin, poignant notes of the robin in September, the last song of summer.

In April it is the willow warbler's tumbling song that cheers me the most. It is one of the surest signs of a turn towards warm spring weather, and always sounds to me as if the bird were leaning back against the new shoots and whistling at the sky with sheer relief.

Some songs can conjure up a whole cameo of memories. This for instance, from the trilling of common sandpipers . . . a late April dawn in Abernethy Forest in the Highlands. Walking through the native pinewoods to the osprey hide at Loch Garten. Roe deer and red squirrels, and a capercaillie blustering on a track. And echoing across the Loch, the liquid calls of sandpipers and the last whooper swans, and the wild banshee cries of black-throated divers.

It is remarkable how many birdsongs seem to have been scored to fit their surroundings, as if they were natural background music. The lilting of curlews over an empty moor. The shivering song of a wood warbler by a garlic-edged Welsh stream. And, later in the year, the jangling of the corn buntings over baked wheatfields. Is it just familiarity that makes these associations seem so apt? Or do birdsongs have a kind of ecological design that we can dimly sense? I suspect that we respond not simply to birdsong but *through* it. The bird becomes a medium, another channel for experiencing those senses of season and territory that still survive within us.

April 1

A natural folly in Hardings Wood. A primrose-yellow brimstone butterfly perfectly still on a primrose flower.

April 11

Railway embankments at Harrow. A gaudy and cosmopolitan show of hardy flowers, most of them plants which have escaped from gardens and become naturalised on these line-side herbaceous borders: flowering American currants, German irises, red, white and blue Spanish bluebells. A little further on there are thickets of lilac in full flower, merging with the native sycamore and willow scrub.

April 15 *Suffolk Coast*

A warm day, with a thin, low cloud cover. There has been fine weather for some time, and I am surprised that there aren't more migrant birds in evidence. At the back of Walberswick marsh, I glimpse a large, dark bird of prey – a marsh harrier, I think – spiralling up in a thermal. Just below cloud level (its wings were cutting through the lowest wisps) it is suddenly surrounded by a milling swarm of perhaps fifty swallows and martins, which I see come down *out* of the clouds to mob it. The whole throng sweeps slowly away to the north until it is lost in the haze.

A few minutes later I see what I think is the harrier reappearing, flying back at the same height. But it is a different bird, a big sparrowhawk or a goshawk. Again the hirundines come down to harass it.

Odd to think of these normally public birds moving about like this, beyond sight. Perhaps they arrived just as discreetly and have been feeding at high altitudes. (In hot weather especially, martins and swifts will follow rising insect swarms – 'aerial plankton' – up to several thousand feet.)

April 16 *Barking, Suffolk*

A swarm of primroses and cowslips in the unmown church-yard (including some *orange* cowslips) and all manner of hybrids and colour varieties between them.

April 19

Wind veers round to the south-east, and temperatures climb above 20°C (68°F). Cherry and blackthorn are coming into full bloom together. Brimstones and comma butterflies are out. Down in the valley of the winterbourne two swallows coast past the black poplar. The first of the year.

APRIL 21 *North Norfolk Coast*

A hot clear day. I walk along the sea-wall from Burnham Deepdale to Burnham Norton, and watch the migrants trickling in : swallows, martins, the first little terns and a ring ouzel, bound perhaps for the Yorkshire Dales. Suddenly, from a ditch a few yards in front of me, a bittern flaps heavily into the air, a flurry of chequered, owlish plumage and discomfiture.

Only a few now nest along the coast, and I have never seen one so close. Its bill is gaping wide – and I realise I am gaping too.

APRIL 24

Seven in the evening at home. There is flash of black and white outside the sitting-room window and a fleeting sound like pebbles being shaken together. The house martins are back. For the next hour they dash back and forth in front of the house, swooping up from time to time to examine last year's nest. It is still intact, tucked into the corner of a west-facing upstairs window, but has been worn down to soup-bowl size during the winter.

By dusk they seem to have decided that it will serve for another year, and we know that we have house-guests for the next five months. They demand nothing from us but tolerance, and in return are wonderfully entertaining famil-iars, energetic, inventive and touchingly devoted.

But they are also a mixed blessing. Once the young have hatched I find it hard to concentrate on my own business. I suffer agonies when the parents are caught away from the nest in storms, and something close to rapture at that moment when the young take their first flight.

APRIL 25

The Chiltern woods look as ornate and colourful from the outside as they do from inside. Cherry and blackthorn blossom have peaked together, and form two tiers of white round many woodland edges. A third is forming at their bases, where the fallen flower petals have settled.

APRIL 26 *Oxford*

A perfect spring day, and city and university alike are in festive mood. People are picnicking in the parks and lounging in the streets. There are five-legged races and croquet matches on college lawns.

The circular walk round Magdalen Meadows is breathtaking. The snowberry thickets have been cut back, and daffodils, primroses and sheets of wide-open *Anemone blanda* are rippling over the river banks. In the meadow itself the snake's-head fritillaries are dense enough to colour whole sheets of the grass purple.

FLOWER OF THE MONTH

In his book *A Herbal Of All Sorts* (1959) Geoffrey Grigson made a list of 'county flowers', in which he suggested that English counties might follow the example of the American states in each choosing an emblematic bloom. His criteria were that the chosen species should all be 'locally abundant, or frequent; and . . . showy (Cornish moneywort would not do for Cornwall)'. Many of his choices – wild daffodil for

View across Magdalen Meadow

Gloucestershire, bird's-eye primrose for Yorkshire, mistletoe for Herefordshire – would be on most botanophiles' lists of the great local landscape plants; and many figure here as flowers of the month.

Grigson's choice for Essex was the March–April flowering oxlip, *Primula elatior*, a speciality of ancient woods (see p. 16) in central East Anglia, where it sometimes grows in huge colonies. The oxlip occurs in Suffolk and Cambridgeshire (as well as in a few 'outlier' colonies in Norfolk, Hertfordshire and Buckinghamshire), but it has special associations with Essex, since this is where the plant was 'discovered' in the 1840s.

It is remarkable that such a handsome and locally abundant flower took so long to be recognised as a distinct species. Traditionally the name 'oxlip' referred to the much more widespread (though always less numerous) hybrid between the primrose and the cowslip. This is probably the species that Shakespeare refers to as the 'bold oxlip' in *The Winter's Tale*. (The hybrid's flowers – upright and spread at the end of the stalk – are certainly bolder than those of the true oxlip, whose smaller blooms droop more closely together and all face the same way.)

It is hard to understand how experienced botanists came to assume these two plants were simply different varieties of the hybrid species, especially as the true oxlip grew in colonies millions-strong in its heartland. But finally two Essex botanists, George Gibson and Henry Doubleday, established the oxlip's true identity. Doubleday studied the colonies round Great Bardfield, a village on the boulder-clay near Thaxted, and concluded that 'they cannot be hybrids, for the primrose does not exist in the parish and these oxlips grow by the thousand in the meadow and in moist woody places adjoining; in one instance a meadow of about two acres is entirely covered by them, being a mass of yellow bloom'. *Primula elatior* was subsequently named the Bard-field oxlip after the location in which it was 'discovered'.

Sadly the Bardfield meadows have gone, along with most of the unimproved grassland in East Anglia, and oxlips are now found almost exclusively in woodland habitats. But there is one happy feature of the Essex colonies that is worth remarking. They show a distinct preference for open, well-walked woods on the fringes of towns. Out in the deep countryside – in Suffolk especially – many of the ancient farm copses where the oxlips grow have been given over to pheasant shooting. They are dark, uncut places where oxlips hang on, but are reluctant to flower. When they do, the buds are promptly chewed off by pheasants and camp-following pigeons.

By contrast, parish copses are usually blessed with well-lit paths and glades, and an increasing number close to Essex towns and villages have seen coppicing (see p. 19) revived. Oxlips often abound along the well-lit edges of public foot-paths and picnic sites, and even under bramble patches. They are, in Essex, splendidly civic plants as well as beautiful ones.

MAY

Ramsons growing in hollow lane, Selborne.

May 1 *Padstow, Cornwall*

The 'Obby 'Oss ceremony on May Day, the most powerful of
the surviving spring rites.

The town is quite clear of traffic, and near the centre the
houses are decked out with sycamore boughs and flags. The
local people who are going to follow the two 'Osses are
dressed in white, with spring flowers (mostly cowslips)
pinned to their shirts or hats, and red-and-white or blue-
and-white spotted handkerchiefs round their necks.

In the middle of the morning the 'Obby 'Osses come out of
their headquarters in the Golden Lion Inn, and you hear the
first chanted choruses of the hypnotic song that will ring
round the streets all day, against a rhythmic background of

51

drums and accordions. The 'Oss is a spectacular beast, made from a hoop-shaped frame about six-feet round and covered with black tarpaulin, which completely covers the 'rider' inside. In front is a small wooden horse's head with snapping jaws, but the horseman's own head is covered with a fearsome conical mask. The most important of the 'Oss's attendants is the Teaser, who carries a club and is dressed in bizarre clothes that vary from year to year.

Two 'Osses and attendants, the red and the blue teams, circle round the town all day, whirling and singing, stopping frequently to serenade particular houses. Every so often the 'Oss 'dies', sinking to the ground while the Teaser strokes his head. The song changes to a different, dirge-like rhythm with inherited and now incomprehensible words. Then suddenly the old beat is picked up again, and the 'Oss leaps up and dances away, resurrected.

So it goes on throughout the day, until the two 'Osses join up in the evening by the maypole in the market square.

It is a dramatic and emotional ritual, and even the most sceptical find themselves carried away by it. Is this just a consequence of the intoxicating music? Or can ancient rituals, even in these sceptical times, continue to tap our atavistic links with nature and the seasons?

MAY 2 *Oxfordshire*

The first swift rockets through the high fog outside Thame. A latish date, but part of the appeal of swifts is that they are beyond tidy accounting. They are natural dare-devils, living on a tightrope between earth and sky, between tropical high spirits and draining northern chills. A restrained, predictable swift, a package-tourist swift which arrived on the same day each spring would be only half the bird we love.

Later, in the Grendon Woods on the Oxfordshire border, a storm blows up, with thunderclaps and hail driven on a bitter north-west wind. Rooks dash back to the meagre cover of their nests in Doddershall Wood. There is one sitting tight in the tree I am sheltering under, with just its tail visible – a heart-tugging sight.

MAY 3

A pair of house martins sit side by side in the shell of last-year's nest like two gossips on a bench, chattering ceaselessly to each other.

Martins nest-building

MAY 6 *Chess Valley, Chilterns*

The day of the spring quickening. Many cuckoos calling from the water meadows, and cuckoo flower in sudsy pink bloom beneath them. Lapwings on eggs in the spring wheat, pink coralroot and bluebell in flower under beech leaves that are still translucent against the pure blue sky. Strolling in these woods, with the turquoise light and rippling shadows on the trunks, is like walking underwater.

Towards the end of the afternoon, mixed flocks of swifts and house martins begin drifting in very high from the south-east.

MAY 7

A balmy night with a three-quarter moon. We walk across the fields to the pub for the first out-of-doors evening drink of the year. The cow parsley and early May blossom are glowing almost luminously in the moonlight.

MAY 8 *Chilterns*

Great storms, followed by oppressive, sulphurous air. Torrents of floodwater and flints have swept into the lanes. The woods are transformed into a rainforest, and a hot mist seeps up through the young beech leaves.

MAY 11 *London*

Another humid, misty, claustrophobic day. I console myself on the train journey home by trying to spot swifts through a single frame of the window (commuting makes one prone to such kindergarten diversions). By the time I am home, I have seen ten separate packs rocketing out of the fog, skidding over rows of terraced houses in Kilburn, slaloming between gasometers in Watford, coursing the gravel pits near Hemel Hempstead. I get off the train hugely refreshed by the thought that at least one group of living things believes it is still spring.

May 12 *Tring Reservoirs, Hertfordshire*

The weather has turned cooler and windier, and there are thousands of swifts and hirundines hunting out over the open water. The swifts are awesome to watch, seeming to fly equally fast with or against the wind, and able to sheer off into a run across the air-flow – almost an aerial skid – by a quick tilt of the wings. Given the speed at which they travel, their timing is astonishing. They glance past tree-tops and rise just clear of the reservoir banks after a flat-out race a foot above the water surface. They are flying as exuberantly and freely as in warm weather, and I wonder if they even notice the conditions. I have read that they will sometimes travel five hundred miles on the edge of a pressure front to escape cold or high winds.

May 14 *Hollow Lanes, Selborne*

Flowers from all kinds of habitat blooming together in these warm and sheltered sunken ways. Cuckoo flowers and golden saxifrage in the damper patches; early purple orchids, red campion, herb Paris with its extraordinary crown of golden stamens, a *grey* germander speedwell, arched stems of Solomon's seal, sweet woodruff, all set in drifts of wild garlic.

Later in the summer the lanes become the equivalent of woodland ravines. Ferns flourish in the humid shade.

Clouds of insects hover in the still air, and are preyed on by warblers and flycatchers swooping out of the ancient maples that cling to the banks.

MID-MAY

Nightingale moon. The first nightingales touch down in this country round about mid-April, after their long flights from tropical Africa. These early birds, mainly solitary males, take up territories in woodland thickets and dense hedgerows, and only occasionally break into short bursts of song. The migration of the females lags behind that of the males by a week or two, and reaches a peak during the May full moon, which provides ideal conditions for night-time navigation. So it may not be too fanciful to think of the male's loud vigils at this moment of the year as serenades. They are sung out under moonlit skies that are probably more full of female nightingales than at any other time.

The male birds continue to sing until the middle of June, but more are imagined than are actually heard. A bird singing during the night is not necessarily a nightingale, and they can be just as vocal during the day. But once you have heard one clearly, there is little chance of being mistaken again, or of being surprised that it has become our most celebrated songster. The song is not as rhythmic as a thrush's or as varied as a blackbird's, and its qualities are as much operatic as strictly musical, dependent on tone and timing, and exquisitely dramatic silences and reprises.

Nightingales are finicky birds, restricted by climate and geography, and there is little chance of hearing one north of a line drawn between Dorset and the Wash. They rarely nest more than four hundred feet above sea level – or, it seems, out of reach of oak leaves and nettles. Their favourite habitats are overgrown woods, especially close to water, dense blackthorn hedges and coppice regrowth between four and seven years old.

Yet where conditions are right for them – especially in south-east England – they can be locally frequent, and in parts of Kent and Sussex it is still possible to have the unforgettable experience of hearing half-a-dozen singing at once. The best also seem to have an uncanny knack of choosing natural amphitheatres for their performances (or at least tempting you to choose a good seat to listen from). I have listened to them by a pond in the Suffolk Breckland, singing against the howl of F-111s from Lakenheath air-base; lounged in a Hampshire green lane at midnight while four chorused together in the dense double boundary hedge; and wondered at them whistling into the wind from brambly shell-holes in the Tyneham ranges in south-west Dorset.

MAY 16 *Dyfed, West Wales*

A passing red kite stops the traffic in Devil's Bridge. It is sailing like a galleon above the narrow village street, more high-masted than a buzzard or harrier. When it catches the sun, its plumage seems tortoiseshell, a chequer of dark grey, white and ginger.

MAY, THIRD WEEK *Dungeness, Kent*

The ancient shingle system south of Romney Marsh is one of the topographical wonders of Britain, and, in winter, can look as if it deserves everything that has been visited upon it. The Ness tails off into the Channel like a collapsed scree slope. It is a harsh, windswept, infertile place, and, like most 'wastelands', has become a gathering ground for all kinds of flotsam and jetsam that isn't welcome inland. Two nuclear power stations squat next to a shanty town of holiday shacks and bungalows. There is gravel digging and water extraction. Small-arms fire from MoD ranges echoes through an ancient, stunted holly wood. Underneath it all the shingle bedrock is being shifted slowly but inexorably eastwards by the sea.

I am here on a dustily hot day in early May, pleased to see migrant black terns wafting over the bright blue water which fills the old diggings, though almost any patch of coastal fresh water would do for them. At the top of a ridge a more extraordinary view opens out, not of a flat block of shingle but of long ridges, topped with vegetation and curving gently away towards the point of the Ness. This is what makes Dungeness unique. For the past five thousand years sea currents have torn shingle out of beaches to the west and deposited them on the far side of this tooth-like promontory. And, for reasons buried deep in long-term tidal patterns and the physics of pebble movement, the sea doesn't dump the shingle at a steady rate, but rhythmically, as ridges. A ridge reaches its maximum height and breadth after about ten to fifteen years, and once it is stable, wave action starts building the next. There are more than four hundred in the Dungeness system, which makes it one of the most extensive and exquisitely formed in the world. I understand now why an aerial picture of the headland reminded me of the annual rings on an immense tree stump.

The vegetation of the ridges has its own pattern of succession, beginning with isolated clumps of sea kale on the newest ridges, and maturing as dense, heathy mixtures of stagshorn lichens, mosses, and scarce and curious flowers like Nottingham catchfly and prostrate broom. And it has an insect population to match, with an extraordinary profusion of bumblebees, moths and beetles, and a miniature pastoral society of lichen-grazers.

What is odd is that, against all the rules, this succession doesn't usually end up as woodland. There are patches of blackthorn and elder, and, deep inside the MoD ranges at Holmstone, a community of ancient prostrate hollies. But over most of the shingle, conditions are either too frugal for the development of trees, or the ridges are too short lived. Already the oldest are being eaten away by the same tidal movements that created them, and being redeposited to the east of the Ness.

We make slow but sonorous progress, crunching on lichen dried to a crisp by the drought, and clattering on the pebbles. Locals used to travel on a kind of wooden ski, which was kinder to the ridges as well as to calf muscles. Every stray shell from the ranges and each passing vehicle leaves an ineradicable dent on the surface. Even footfalls irreversibly disturb lichen-crusted stones that may have been in the same position for thousands of years. My companion, who has been coming here since the 1950s, is uneasily aware that many of the dim footprints here are his. 'It is,' he says, 'like walking on the surface of the moon.'

Dungeness has many friends who wish it could become a National Nature Reserve. It could be a salutary example, the first such reserve with mobile boundaries, and a reminder that nature is not a fixed, marketable commodity but something mutable and alive. It would point up the facile injustice of that word 'wasteland' too. Gravel could always be dug from alternative sites – offshore, for instance, or under surplus farmland – if we so chose, and were prepared to pay more for it. But natural systems like Dungeness are irreplaceable cultural and scientific resources, immense memory banks of the ways in which our thin skin of inhabitable earth goes on evolving.

MAY 20 *Roydon Wood, Hampshire*

Woodcrawling in one of the most southerly woods in Britain, on the banks of the Beaulieu River. It is outside the New Forest boundaries and free of grazing, and young trees are regenerating almost as freely as they do across the Channel. There are young maples, hazels, beech, alder buckthorn, even wild service-tree seedlings. Flowers that are particular about their habitats further north are mixed in wonderful abandon here: spurge laurel, orpine (not yet in flower), woodruff, and, in more open, heathy patches, the rare New Forest lungwort.

MAY 21

A pure May evening, with a sky the colour of copper. May blossom in full bloom, and so dense that its weight is bending the hawthorn branches. Its scent, mixed with the tang of cow parsley, floats in through the closed car windows.

MAY 24

The martins have begun repairing their nest after days of earnest conversation. They start in the early morning, carrying a very dark mud from a source no more than two minutes' flying time away. They work methodically, first filling in the holes developed from the wear-and-tear of last year's two broods, then laying on a single line of mud along the broken rim of the nest. They arrive with beaks full of mud, and sometimes a little dry grass, lay it in place, and then dibble it home with a rapid hammering movement of the bill. Occasionally the technique changes, and they use slower movements with an open bill, squeezing the mud pellets into place. Gradually they work the line of new mud into a gentle curve, building up the edges of the entrance hole faster than its base.

LATE MAY

The heat has brought on a profusion of insects. In my wood there are some mysterious moths which hover and dance all day in swarms over the tops of the cherry trees. They have immense antennae, many times longer than their bodies, and, at a distance, look uncannily like the creatures on Space Invaders screens.

After much fruitless bookworming I identify them as longhorn moths, and pick up a few bare facts about their extraordinary life cycle. They begin as leaf-mining caterpillars, before making portable shells for themselves out of chewed scraps of leaves and crawling about the trees like miniature arboreal tortoises.

Later comes the Invasion of the Pollen Beetles. They had been massing quietly in the oil-seed rape flowers, and now they are pouring into the surrounding countryside in astronomical numbers. *Megalithes aeneas* are tiny, rotund creatures that have a liking for mass tribal gatherings and a touching devotion to the colour of their birthplace. They swarm over mustard-yellow T-shirts and ochre handbags. They sunbathe on half-eaten apples. A golfing friend who uses yellow balls reported finding them blackened by swarms of the insects by the time he reached the green.

I wish we knew more about insects, and didn't regard them as only of value when they are 'used' by other crea-

tures. Contrary to usual impressions about the 'pyramid of
life', the earth's insect species (maybe twenty-five million)
outnumber plants by twenty to one. They exploit every
possible niche, even the malodorous flowers of a loathsome
arable crop. They are brilliant, inventive, prolific and sometimes (think of the mayfly) as seemingly frivolous and
wasteful as disposable tissues. I suspect we could learn much
from them about adaptation to an unstable world.

MAY, LAST WEEK *Dowrog Common and St David's Head,
Pembrokeshire*

We set out from our quiet cottage on the common (its
granite walls are two feet thick and cut out even the dawn
clamour from the local curlews and oystercatchers) for an
expedition to the St David's peregrine eyrie.

A local farmer (they are very protective of the birds)
realises that we are not collectors, and shows us how to find
the narrow cliff path. Halfway up the long climb, we see the
male peregrine coming down. It is gliding about a hundred
feet above us, but close enough for me to see the black
moustachial stripes for the first time.

We eventually reach the path and head west. At first the
cliff-top flowers are sensational – drifts of pink thrift, blue
spring squill and sheep's-bit, white sea campion and ox-eye
daisy and yellow kidney vetch. Then the vegetation changes
to a mix of heather, broom and gorse, in full flower and
smelling of coconut and peaches in the sun.

After half an hour's slow walking we are about two
hundred and fifty feet above sea level, and spot another
peregrine at eye level. A much browner bird, probably a
female; she spots us and does a short, smart, crossbow stoop
out of sight behind the cliff. Further on there are choughs,

sporting about the cliff like immense black butterflies, and stonechats clucking on the gorse. It is hard at times to tell their alarm calls from the furious popping of the gorse pods in the sun.

But when we arrive at the presumed site of the eyrie, we meet two friends, who had set out before us, staring gloomily at a pile of sticks on the facing cliff. There is absolutely nothing in it, and for a while we fear that the chicks have been stolen or fallen out. But, on closer inspection, the nest seems anciently abandoned, with no sign of prey, droppings or occupation.

Later we learn that it is a deserted raven's nest, to which we may well have been directed as a deliberate piece of misinformation. We are so relieved, we do not mind that our expedition has been a failure. The peregrines themselves continue to delight us for the remainder of the week, having spectacular dog-fights with buzzards and crows often right over our cottage.

May 30

Back in the Chilterns the house martins' plumage is begin-ning to look mud-spattered. They are reaching the end of their repair work and have changed their technique again. One bird appears to have taken on the role of bricklayer and the other of hod-carrier. The carrier brings quite large pellets of mud, and leaves them on the advancing edge of the nest. The other, working from *inside* the nest, moves mud to where it is needed on the closing edges of the entrance hole and then dibbles it in place. They stop building at about noon, giving each new layer of mud time to dry before applying the next. I never cease to be amazed by the way in which their building instincts can produce the unfamiliar tricks necessary to repair a randomly damaged nest.

FLOWER OF THE MONTH

Bird's-eye primrose, one of the most exquisite of all our native wild flowers. It is alpine in habit, with a posy of coral-pink flowers carried above a rosette of dusty grey-green leaves. The great plant collector Reginald Farrer, who had seen hill species all over the world, still rated this little primula from his native West Riding above all others.

Bird's-eye grows in damp limestone grassland in north-west England, especially on peaty soils that are moistened by limestone flushes. I saw my first on Shap Fell, on a high pasture studded with rushes and red rattle, where they were growing on ground which seemed to be raised above the level of the waterlogged peat. Their scattering over the pasture followed exactly the marks of the lime-rich water moving close to the surface of the peat.

Since then I have seen them growing on the banks (and miniature islands) of Yorkshire streams, tracing the line of water seepage down steep limestone hills, even gathering in pockets of low-lying peat where water drains from the road.

Bird's-eye Primroses, North Yorkshire

JUNE

Wild strawberry growing in rock crevices

Most of our countryside puts on its best finery in June, but for the Yorkshire Dales this is a supreme moment, when the combination of rock and wild flowers make it Britain's most festive landscape.

It took me a while to see this for myself. I'd never felt easy in the barren openness of the uplands, and it was not until early middle age that I realised the Dales were neither barren nor lonely. But even then it was a cautious, occasional affair. It was the flowers that captivated me first – coral-pink bird's-eye primroses among bleached sheep bones and rock-roses in hanging gardens along the limestone terraces. Then the sugar-loaf swell of Ingleborough hill, that seems to swim into view wherever you are in the Dales, and which the locals simply call 'The Hill', as if there isn't another worth mentioning. It was the limestone rock itself, the raw stuff of the place, that clinched it. Perhaps it has been a case of finding sermons in stones; but the landscape up here is too frank and easy-going to be preachy, and historical romance is much more in its line.

Limestone is the bedrock of the Dales. It shapes their way of life and gives the landscape colour and liveliness and a kind of geographical logic. It is warm, adaptable, ingenuous. Auden called it a 'stone that responds'. It wears its history like lines on a face, and almost everywhere you walk in the Dales, over cracked limestone pavements, down dried-out gulches and underground river systems, you will be exploiting the fact that this rock, formed out of the skeletons of myriads of sea creatures, is weathered and shaped by water like no other.

My first walk in the Dales was a riverside trek, up the lower reaches of the Wharf. It was a placid enough stroll to start with, but where the river burst through into the limestone, just north of Grassington, the whole landscape came alive. The river frothed, dippers bobbed on flood-smoothed boulders, purple veins of wild thyme ran down the cracks in the rock and almost into the water.

The true Dales are the valleys cut through the soft rock by rivers and glaciers, and they are lined with spectacular limestone terraces, sculptured and layered by the weather. Many of the Dales' valleys – in Langstrothdale, Dentdale and Littondale especially – are still lined with flowery hay meadows. They are best for walking on June evenings, when the sun is slanting through the buttercups and wild cranesbills. But there is another waterside walk which I will only say is along a half-buried beck between Fountains Fell and Malham, since much of the thrill is in finding it for yourself and wondering if you are ever going to get out. You walk past deep pools and cascades of redeposited limestone (tufa) and along precipitous ledges lined with wild yew trees, with oystercatchers and redshank piping your progress.

Yet the Dales are a landscape of foreground detail as well as views, and it is worth resisting the temptation to hike non-stop. Sit down by any stretch of running water, and watch trapped pebbles grinding out the shape that is stamped like a footprint throughout limestone country. Sit anywhere, for that matter, and watch the whole landscape evolving. Scree settles, splinters of rock crack off. Sometimes limestone seems light enough to move in the wind. It certainly shifts in storms, when flash flooding fills the underground caverns and comes bursting through the sides of hills, carrying gushes of rock and soil with it.

The limestone pavements are amongst the region's most remarkable water sculptures. They are flat plains of limestone, smoothed by glaciers and then cracked and eroded into fissured blocks by rainfall. In the cracks – known as 'grikes' – an astonishing mixture of woodland and alpine flowers grow. Lily of the valley is one of the specialities, and can scent the air for a hundred yards around on warm June days.

The permanent waterfalls are worth a meditative linger, too. At Weathercote, there is one *inside* a cave. Turner painted this is 1816, amazed by the spectacle of an underground waterfall, which, because the cave roof had collapsed, seemed to tumble out of a pool of sunlight. On his second visit it was raining so hard that the cave was half full of water, and he had to be content with sketching from the top. But he added one of the rainbows that are always visible when you look up through the spray from below.

He also painted the huge drop at Hardraw Force, the highest unbroken fall in England. In the hard winter of 1739 Hardraw became a column of ice, solid enough for the people of Hawes to dance round it. These days the natural amphitheatre round it is better known as the site of a wonderful piece of Yorkshire whimsy, a brass-band competition, held amongst an echoing clamour of jackdaws and rushing water.

Moughton Fell, an immense plateau of shattered limestone between Ingleborough and the quarries at Ribblesdale, is both walking and meditating country. I once found a fresh peregrine kill by a beck at the bottom of the fell, a racing pigeon with its identification ring incongruously bright amongst the bloody feathers. I sat and gazed at that unsettling number, and its evidence of the individuality of life. The Dales' landscape is like that, specific, idiosyncratic – a region, Auden wrote, 'Of short distances and definite places'. I saw tiny clumps of bird's-eye primroses growing on islands in the beck, out of the way of nibbling sheep, and, in the drystone wall, layers of a local rock known as banded whetstone. Wading in the stream I found more of it and had a sudden, pleasant fantasy of being a gold-panner.

The Dales aways have that human dimension, despite their exhilarating sense of wildness and freedom. On many of the local farms and cottages you will find a kind of vernacular sculptury decorating the walls and roofs – 'found stones' picked out for their likeness to animals or pieces of furniture.

Even the huge quarry faces, rightly regarded as abominations in a National Park, look uncannily like the natural terraces that line the valleys. Limestone has this knack of mellowing outrages, softening grey skies and providing a tonic for natives and pilgrims alike. Whether you are amongst shepherds, weekend potholers or drystone wallers, there is a feeling here, as in few other places in England, that people are working with the landscape not against it.

June 1 (1984)

Massive local hailstorm. The first portents are a TV blackout and ominous pitch-dark clouds; then torrential rain turning in a matter of minutes into sheets of hail the size of raisins. In a friend's house the stones are rasping the soot out of the chimney and falling as black ice in the grate. Visibility is almost nil, and downhill roads are soon carrying torrents of floodwater and ice. In the garden most big-leaved plants look as if they have been peppered with grape shot, and piles of stones – a foot deep in places – linger under the hedges till the next day.

June 6 *Cressbrook Dale, Derbyshire*

In a remote corner of this Dale I stumble on a kind of Lost World, a relic of the vegetation that advanced across Britain after the retreat of the ice. It is like following a trail through prehistoric succession; first open limestone grassland, with early purple orchids and meadow saxifrage and cowslips, then burnet rose scrub, with lily of the valley and scrambling bloody cranesbill, and then an airy Nordic grove of hazel and aspen over a sloping meadow. In it were species that must have grown together after the retreat of the glaciers, plants from woodland, wetland, acid and alkaline soils, but which eight thousand years of forest clearance and cultivation have pushed towards their own specialised habitats.

Early June

Songs of summer. By now the melodious choruses of the spring woodland songbirds have been augmented by the drowsy, repetitive calls of birds of open country. Nightjars churr, whitethroats crackle, turtle doves purr. As in spring, their songs seem to be perfectly scored for long, hot dusty days. Two in particular summon up very special moments . . .

A baking day in the Chilterns. Lolling on a chalk down overlooking a sweep of unsprayed corn. Fragrant orchids and the scents of crushed thyme and salad burnet. A family of fox cubs playing amongst the poppies. Then quite unexpectedly, a quail begins to call, a distant, insistent sound like a scythe being sharpened. Then another joins in – the only ones I have ever heard in this country and sounding like an elegy for this miniature pastoral scene.

An Irish hay meadow near the Burren in County Clare, still twilit at midnight. Cuckoos are calling, but the corncrakes that traditionally nest here seem disinclined to join them. We try to start them up by rubbing a metal comb against the radiator of our car, which makes a passable imitation of the grating call that gives the bird its Latin name *Crex crex*, but which also causes the car lights to go off and on in the same rhythm. Quite soon the corncrakes begin to answer, and the meadows ring with our joint chorus, a bizarre *son et lumière*.

JUNE 12 *Suffolk*

Out looking for nightjars. The first one starts promptly forty minutes after sunset and soon moves onto a telegraph wire to churr. Then it vanishes and I hear nothing for a while except their 'quik' flight calls and some curious thumpings. At first I imagine these are rabbits in the undergrowth. Then two nightjars begin gliding just a foot or two above the bracken in an exultant courtship chase, and I can see that the thumping noise is their wings being clapped above their backs. They fly so close to me that I can see the whiskers under their wide bills and the white spots on their wings. They circle round me, clapping and darting up, a bewitching vision in the half light.

These were some of the most thrilling and beguiling night-jars I have experienced, but I am not sure if they were the first I had seen. They are one of a small company of birds that have always haunted my dreams and pensive moments, so that I can scarcely untangle which birds are real and which are flights of fancy.

Nightjars, dusk-haunters, moth-gulpers, fern-owls, have always been birds of dream and myth. For centuries they were believed to suck the teats of goats, to infect young calves with a fatal disease known as 'puckeridge', to produce their churring song by strange vibrations of their feathers.

Gilbert White was one of the first naturalists to look clearly and affectionately at them. One evening in the 1760s, he and a group of friends were taking tea in the Hermitage on Selborne's wooded common, when a nightjar settled on the roof. It began to churr, and the company were 'all struck with wonder to find that the organs of that little animal, when put in motion, gave sensible vibration to the whole building'. He was sure that the note was produced in its windpipe, 'just as cats purr'.

White saw these 'nocturnal swallows' as being evocative of warm summer nights in the same way that swallows themselves capture the feel of long summer days. That part of their magical aura will, with luck, never be exorcised. Although I can't be sure that I recall my first nightjar, many of them have been memorable, and seemed to conjure up moments when it was as if a bubble of the hot south had been transported to England. One evening on a heath near Walberswick, in Suffolk, a nightjar sat and churred in a dead oak, accompanied for nearly a quarter of an hour by a filibustering nightingale in the blackthorn bush below. In the New Forest I have seen fern-owls dust-bathing on the unmade roads, and, in the newly-felled areas of the Breckland conifer plantations in East Anglia, they fill the ferny clearings with that ventriloquial reeling, and seem to warm the barrenness back to life.

Alas, the heaths and their 'night insects' are everywhere in decline, and nightjars with them. Yet they have been one of the beneficiaries of our recent warm summers, and there are still maybe three or four thousand pairs whose summer twilight churrings can seem like the quintessence of the heathland. On the right kind of warm June nights it can be an unforgettable experience: the light drains from the sky, the reeling seeps in from what seems like immense foreign distances, then swells until it reverberates inside your head. Abruptly it stops. A branch seems to break free and float towards you, and suddenly the fern-owl is 'glancing' (White's word cannot be bettered) over the tops of the trees, narrow wings arched above its back and bouncing as if it were being tugged on a string towards the night sky.

June 13 *Norfolk Fenland*

An evening trip to the poplar plantation where Britain's only sizeable colony of golden orioles breeds. A very airy, French-looking wood, with dappled light even at this midsummer season. We do not spot the orioles this time. They are always shy birds, and, here, their olive-green plumage merges with the pale green poplar leaves. But we hear their song from the tree tops: soft, echoing, liquid – a fenbell.

JUNE 19 *North Norfolk*

The marshes at Burnham Norton are buzzing with life on this brilliant day in the heart of the breeding season. Reed warblers chattering every few yards in the dykes, yellow wagtails nesting close to wallowing cattle; a nervous pair of avocets; harriers soaring over the reed beds, and everywhere the air teeming with martins and swallows.

JUNE 20

In a rare downpour a bedraggled carrion crow sits in a garden birch tree, points its head towards the leaden skies and lets the rain drip into its open bill.

JUNE 23 *Underbarrow Scar, Lancashire*

Wonderful limestone flora: prostrate juniper bushes, small meadow rue, bloody cranesbill and hoary rock-rose. Amongst them are wild strawberries with ripe fruit made warm and liquid by lying in the sun on the bare white rock. They dissolve into beads of fragrance in the mouth, and I have a vague memory of a sixteenth-century recipe for a strawberry biscuit, made from fine sugar and 'almond milk' and cooked by putting the mixture on a dish in the sun.

JUNE 24

Engrossed in a Wimbledon quarter-final on the TV, I become aware of a great hubbub outside, and see that the parent martins are flying distractedly back and forth across the garden. I rush out and find a chunk torn out of the front of the nest, the adults fled and the whole newly-hatched brood – four blind three-day-old nestlings – scattered dead and bloodstained about the drive. I have no idea what happened, whether it was an attack by a woodpecker, or a sparrow, perhaps. I am heartbroken and bury the little corpses under a rose bush near the wall on which they were hatched. But in the evening the parents return, and spend most of the night in deep debate inside the nest. The next day they work furiously on repairs, building up the hole so tightly they can barely get in themselves. Within two weeks they are sitting on another clutch of eggs.

JUNE 29 *Cumbria*

Up on the fells above Ambleside, I come across a sundew 'meadow' – a large patch of these insectivorous plants growing together on a flat shelf of peat. It is late evening, and the sticky, red-spined leaves are glowing fuzzily against the setting sun.

In the valley meadows below, the globular flower heads of the great burnet are a deeper, almost venous, blood-red. No wonder that the plant was once used by herbalists for staunching wounds.

JUNE 30 *Cumbria*

Curlews are grazing in the newly-mown hay meadows like sheep on the aftermath. Straggling flocks of young and non-breeding lapwings are migrating south and west. It is the turn of the year.

FLOWER OF THE MONTH

June is the month of wild briars just as much as of garden roses. Our native species are not only a fascinating and beautiful group in their own right, but have played a part in the origins of many cultivated varieties.

The common dog rose, *Rosa canina*, normally pink, sometimes occurs in pure white forms. A chance hybridisation with the field rose, *Rosa arvensis*, was probably the origin of the large-flowered garden variety *Andersonii*. The field rose itself, whose flowers are a more invariable white with showy golden anthers, is a spectacular climber. In woods or tall hedges it will sometimes climb thirty or forty feet, and flower in the canopy like a rainforest creeper. Forms of the field rose and crosses with old-fashioned garden roses were the origin of the now almost vanished group, the double, rambling, fragrant Ayrshire roses.

Rosa tomentosa, the downy rose, with dark pink, velvety flowers is common in the north of Britain. The allied species *Rosa villosa*, is one of the parents of 'Wolley-Dod's Rose' discovered in a Cheshire vicarage garden in 1900. The burnet rose, *Rosa pimpinellifolia*, of sea-cliffs and limestone country, is the most delicate and beautifully scented of all our wild species. It is the basis of the early-flowering *Pimpinellifolia* hybrids that have been a speciality of German rose-breeders. The 'Dunwich Rose', is a prostrate variety discovered on the Suffolk coast. The sweet briar, *Rosa eglanteria*, whose leaves smell of fresh apples, especially after rain, was also once popular amongst rose enthusiasts. Until the early years of this century a dozen or so sweet briar varieties were available, including varieties with double-flowers, marble coloured flowers, and flowers with concave petals.

Antique varieties like this are sometimes rediscovered as

naturalisations or relics in old gardens. The 'Woolverstone Church Rose', a rose of Victorian but otherwise unknown origins, was discovered growing up the wall of a Suffolk church by the distinguished rose-grower Humphrey Brooke. The bush was over a hundred years old but still flowering. (It has one of the strongest scents of any rose, and a blind friend of Brooke's once put his nose in a bloom and said: 'If this scent was available in a bottle it would put every tart in Europe out of business'.) In another Suffolk churchyard is the 'Omar Khayyam Rose', which grows on the tomb of the

Rosa richardii, 'The Holy Rose'

poet Edward FitzGerald in Boulge. It was planted there in 1893 from cuttings taken from the plants on Omar Khayyam's tomb in Nishapur.

My name rose, *Rosa richardii*, has also proved itself a great survivor. It is a species from the Middle East, which has reverted almost to the wild in my garden. Also known as the 'Abyssinian Rose' and the 'Holy Rose', it is one of the oldest of all cultivated roses. Its remains were discovered by Flinders Petrie in an Egyptian tomb, and a painting of it on the murals at Knossos in Crete is the earliest known representation of a rose.

I planted it out of sentimentality for its name and history, thinking that a plant so far away from its native home would grow with a decent restraint. Instead it has spread into a dense thicket many square yards in extent, and has already broken through the fence into my neighbour's rockery. But it is worth it. It survives the hardest of winters, and for six weeks in May and June it is covered with a mass of overlapping, cream-pink blooms. They are so symmetrical as to be almost heraldic.

JULY

Breckland

It is the summer heatwave of 1983, and I am waiting at my home railway station in Hertfordshire when, a few inches above the track, a clouded yellow butterfly flies past, heading determinedly in the direction of London. It isn't just the sight of this scarce immigrant in such an improbable setting that surprises me (quite large numbers have been tempted over from the Continent by the warm weather) so much as its show of purposefulness as it floats along what is a human trackway. This is a butterfly bound for the hot spots.

The railways have much in common with the motorways as refuges for wildlife. They have the same ribbons of embankment scrub and rough grassland, and the same relative freedom from pesticide onslaughts. But more openly than is ever the case from inside a car, the world beyond the train is *displayed* to you. This isn't just a consequence of the greater field of view a carriage window affords, or because you can gaze out with impunity once free of the responsibility of driving. The fact that trains follow absolutely fixed courses – the 'permanent ways' – always gives them the feel of mobile observation platforms. What you lose as a passenger in terms of intimacy and detail, you make up for in a feeling of broad changes in the landscape. Soils and seasons roll past like speeded-up film. It is during spells of regular commuting that you will see most, watching, from the same angle, the same scene change imperceptibly through the year. Buds swell, leaves fall, a flock of birds dashes across the frame.

It is worth developing some watching techniques if you begin to enjoy spotting from trains. If you have a choice, sit on the side of the carriage that is furthest from the embankment. This will give you a wider angle of view and a less rushed image. Don't automatically sit facing the engine. Although this may help you see plants and birds ahead, you can watch them for longer once they are receding. You may find this easier than holding your neck craned back while the object vanishes beyond your peripheral vision. When you have the option, choose slow trains, not just because they are obviously easier to watch from but because the edges of stations (where they will frequently pause) are amongst the best areas for wildlife.

Many of my own seasonal landmarks lie along the twenty-five miles of track between my home and Euston : the first primroses of the year usually appearing in early February on a sheltered, south-facing cutting near Hemel Hempstead ; the first buddleia amongst lineside scrub near Wembley, responding to the higher temperatures of the city. Following the same thermal contours as the clouded yellow butterfly, you can sometimes watch the summer unfold in half an hour. I have known days in late July when the last poppies are in flower at one end of the line and the first michaelmas daisies of autumn at the other, their seasonality underlined by the fact that, notionally, you are running according to a timetable yourself. I find the regularity of these happenstance glimpses oddly reassuring. There go the Watford swifts! Here come the 6.40 Wembley irises – bang on time!

JULY 1 *Upper Teesdale, County Durham*

Natural meadows by the side of the River Tees. Alpine bistort, marsh orchids, wild pansies, growing in grassland which is kept open and treeless by regular flooding.

On the dry shingle beds at the edge of the river there is a colony of shrubby cinquefoil. This is one of only two locations on the British mainland where this handsome plant – probably once common in the open, rocky landscapes of post-glacial Britain – survives.

JULY 2

A clear, hot evening. Sky the colour of bronze. Swifts flying like bats around the canal-side chestnut trees at 10.30 p.m.

JULY 3

A high summer day. Swallows dipping over the ripening barley, whitethroats grating in the hedges. The mixture of smells is extraordinary: broad beans, elder flowers, first toadstools, chaff.

JULY 4 *Barnham Cross Common, the Breckland, Norfolk*

An area of gorse and heath, burned down last year, entirely blanketed by swarms of wild pansies, in every possible combination of colour, from a pure, single lemon, to deep purple.

The Breckland has an extraordinary history. In 1668 the village of Santon Downham was buried under a sandstorm, a blow-out from an inland dune system at Lakenheath Warren, a few miles to the south. By ordinary English standards it was an outlandish occurrence. But not in this 'vast Arabian desert', which straddles the Norfolk–Suffolk borders, and which had long been notorious with travellers. Many used to cross 'the horrible Brandon sands' in the dawn to avoid upsetting the horses, and there was a kind of wooden lighthouse to guide anyone unfortunate enough to be benighted. Seven years after the Santon storm the diarist, John Evelyn, noted that: 'the Travelling Sands have so damaged the country, rolling from place to place, and quite overwhelmed some gentlemen's estates', and urged them to plant 'tufts of firr' to replace the trees that had been removed over the centuries and stabilise the sand.

The Breckland is a prime, home-grown example of what deforestation can lead to. Up to a couple of hundred years ago it was the nearest thing Britain had to a dust-bowl. In parts, this may have been its natural state. The area is defined by deposits of sand and gravel that were washed here by glacial meltwaters, and there may have been areas of especially loose sand on exposed ridges that could never sustain a permanent woodland cover. But most of the open areas were encouraged by human activity. The light soils made forest clearance relatively easy, and in prehistoric times it was one of the most densely populated areas of Britain. Grazing by semi-domesticated cattle soon converted what remained of the woodland to a mixture of wiry grass and heather. A large and sprawling network of trackways and drove roads connected the region with the Icknield Way and trading settlements on the East Anglian coast.

Amongst the most important items of trade ferried along these tracks were worked flints, for use in knives, weapons and farm implements. Flint is abundant throughout East Anglia, but Breckland had some of the best quality, and became a centre for flint-knapping skills. At Grimes Graves, just north of Brandon, there is a prehistoric flint-mine in which, to date, some five hundred and forty shafts have been uncovered.

Early farming itself was a less rewarding business. The thin soils soon began to lose their fertility, and, at some unspecified date, the system that eventually gave the region its name evolved. A field would be cultivated for a few years and then abandoned for as much as twenty to give it time to recover. These long-term fallow plots were named after an Old English term *brek*, meaning a tract of land broken up for cultivation and then allowed to revert.

Sheep grazing was the most sensible use for both the grasslands and the Brecks, and large flocks were roaming the region by Roman times. In the Middle Ages they were joined by rabbits, which were kept in enormous high-banked warrens. By the middle of the eighteenth century there were reckoned to be over fifteen thousand acres of organised warren in the Brecks, and the traveller and agricultural reporter, Arthur Young, quoted the figure of forty thousand rabbits as the production of just one warren.

But as the fashion for 'improvement' gathered pace during the late eighteenth and nineteenth centuries Breckland landowners went in for all manner of schemes to make their local wilderness bear fruit. They planted thickets for pheasants, turnips to enrich the soil, and pine hedges to check the winds. Eventually – with more than a suggestion that poetic justice had been done – Santon Downham rose again as the local headquarters of the Forestry Commission, whose vast pine plantations had become the biggest single enterprise to keep the sand in its place. In the 1940s Lakenheath Warren vanished under the runways of an air base. During the last twenty years all the remaining open dunes have been tidily fenced off and labelled as nature reserves. Breckland has been very nearly brought to heel, but now, for the first time, not everyone feels comfortable about this particular triumph of man over nature.

For much of its recent history Breckland has been re-garded as a classic piece of wasteland, somewhere to lose unpopular and land-hungry activities, such as battle training and commercial forestry. There weren't many other obvious uses for an infertile plain which had the lowest rainfall in Britain, and which was almost devoid of the features usually regarded as characteristic of a picturesque landscape. I doubt if there is another comparable swath of rural England (it covers some four hundred square miles, from Bury St Edmunds in the south to Swaffham in the north) that is so little known and so impatiently rushed through by travellers. When I first began exploring East Anglia thirty years ago it felt like an occupied zone, a hostile territory of barricaded shooting estates and military bases.

Yet you can still catch glimpses of the waste clinging on in the margins. Neolithic flint chips are still turned up in their hundreds in the arable fields. Wild flowers that don't occur again until the East European steppes grow on the road verges. Nightjars find echoes of their ancestral heathland habitats in the new forestry clearings, and churr in ever increasing numbers through the summer dusks. Modern

Breckland may be only a ghost of the old landscape of immense sandy plains and stony scrubland, but when dust-devils are whirling across the carrot fields and through the stunted pine wind-breaks it doesn't seem improbable that flocks of great bustard stalked the plains only a hundred and fifty years ago.

It is, paradoxically, on the Forestry Commission's land that you can come closest to experiencing the feel of the old waste. The Brecks were one of the first areas to be planted up by the Commission in its post-Great-War mission to increase the nation's strategic timber reserve, and by the 1960s much of the countryside here lay under a forbidding and monotonous drape.

Now many of the early plantings are coming round for felling, and the landscape is perceptibly more open. The Commission is promoting conservation on all its estates, and in the Brecks nearly a tenth of the land – almost a full tithe – is dedicated for such purposes. On some sites the Commission is creating large clear fells of thirty hectares or more for reasons that have little to do with timber management. Beyond Emily's Wood, north of Brandon, the Commission has given car-bound travellers on the Swaffham road an idea of what the open prospects of Breckland might once have looked like. Down in Wangford Warren there is a huge clearing specifically for the benefit of nightjars, woodlarks, and hunting goshawks. (A while ago, with typical local opportunism, there was a sign outside a nearby farm which announced 'Goshawks!' as lesser holdings advertise their honey and free-range eggs.)

But much of the rest of Breckland seems to have become a curmudgeonly and inhospitable place. There is almost no-where to walk. The network of ancient tracks that pass across the estates south of Elveden are all blocked off by curt Private signs. Even England's oldest road, the Icknield Way, summarily peters out once it leaves the Forestry Commission's King's Forest. Only the Roman Peddars Way, opened up after long and patient negotiation, is an uninterrupted right of way.

My private fantasy, that the Ministry of Defence will abandon its Battle Training Area, allowing it to become England's first American-style 'roadless area' will doubtless remain a fantasy. But public opinion is changing, and it no longer seems implausible that this gaunt landscape might become a statutory area of Outstanding Natural Beauty, or even a lowland National Park. Options like this are being discussed by those who keep a watchful eye on the Brecks, as is the fact that the area is deteriorating ecologically and may be over-grazed and over-manured. It may be in need of a return to the kind of agriculture that first created the landscape on these impoverished soils – cultivation followed by a long fallow period.

This, ironically, is the kind of system that the Forestry Commission is already following willy-nilly. Its policy of short-term rotations, followed by large clearances, is like a condensation of the ancient farming system here. If it could be persuaded to allow longer periods before replanting it might produce a model for the Brecks, a landscape that, as Thomas Hardy wrote about the heathlands of Dorset, is 'impressive without showiness, emphatic in its admonitions, grand in its simplicity'. And, alternating forest with fallow, it would also be a salutary place for meditating upon the fact that fertility is not something which can be endlessly and relentlessly exploited without, so to speak, a 'break'.

JULY 7 *Studland Heath, Dorset*

A pink crab spider sitting on a marsh orchid flower spike, and looking exactly like one of the blooms – its body colour matching the flower's and its legs mimicking the spurs. Later there is another stranded on a freak *white* marsh orchid – a crab out of water.

July 8

A hooligan swift haunts the garden at lunchtime, careering between the houses, beating up against our wall and clinging to the martins' nest. They fight back, buzzing the intruder and trying to peck its head, but it is too fast and disdainful, and they are like tadpoles worrying a salmon.

July 12

A hot and humid day. In the morning the town swifts are flying high in swarms of between thirty and sixty, milling and gliding in a seemingly haphazard way. They remind me of what scientists call 'Brownian movement' – the random swirling of minute particles suspended in smoke or a liquid.

But then, almost imperceptibly at first, the swarm begins to cohere. Birds join up in accelerating strands. The strands begin to point towards a focus. For a moment all the birds may be flying together. Then, abruptly, they fling apart like a star-burst, with individual birds flying off in all directions.

About an hour before sunset they come down lower and start their more usual evening pack-races. But they stay in these large flocks, so that sometimes a comet's tail of birds rushes across, thirty or more birds jinking and feathering their wings to avoid colliding with each other.

JULY 13

Five different sorts of edible wild fruit ripe in my wood together – redcurrants, strawberries, raspberries, gooseberries and wild cherries.

JULY 14

My annual walk to count the local house martin nests, a personal ritual with its own time-honoured customs.

I have been surveying nests along a fixed three-mile route through the town since the early 1980s, but as the burglar alarms and neighbourhood watch signs have multiplied, so has my self-consciousness. I have tried to work out an inconspicuous technique, sighting the nests from a block or two away, peering down at the pavement for evidence of occupation, and using binoculars only as a last resort. But there are always some late nesters, crammed behind an overhanging eave, for which there is no alternative but the lingering squint up towards the bedroom window; and I am resigned to the fact that, one day, the neighbourhood watch will be watching *me*.

The martins themselves seem similarly discomfited by the new eaves-scape of alarm systems and white pebble dash. They have been declining along my route since 1982, and though drought and the spreading of the desert in the martins' wintering grounds in Africa play a part in this, so do conditions here. The drying out of ponds makes it difficult for the martins to collect mud for nest building. Development of waste ground near houses reduces insect prey.

But there are always fascinating local shifts and increases. They have returned to their traditional site over the Italian hairdresser's, spattering the sunblinds with their droppings, and ignoring the plastic streamers pinned up to deter them. But the colony that used to nest on a pub by the pond – normally a favourite situation in dry summers – has vanished because Virginia creeper has scrambled over the eaves.

JULY 16 *Selborne*

A re-enactment of what Gilbert White saw exactly two hundred years ago on this day: 'Young swallows settle on the grass plots to catch insects'.

JULY 17 *Severn Estuary (2)*

A picnic by the river with a family of friends from Frampton. We set out on a bevy of ancient bicycles, along the flat lanes that meander through the countryside south of the estuary. The air is hot and still between the high hedges and musky with meadowsweet, and we guzzle home-made elderflower cordial. We have the road to ourselves. We freewheel and sing, and spot a pure white sparrow. It feels absurdly like an Enid Blyton Famous Five expedition from the 1950s.

But of the Severn there isn't a sign. Then we swing off the lane and into a field, and there, not a hundred yards away, is the vast openness of the estuary, with a gale funnelling in from the Atlantic. We cower on the clifftop, peg the picnic down with stones and watch the wind rattling the salmon weather-vane on the top of the riverside church at Framilode. Ten miles downstream we can just make out the grey bulk of Berkeley nuclear power station and, exactly opposite, the Forest of Dean, with its Celtic temples and medieval mines. The two miles of white horses between them look unnavigable, even under the July sun.

Then the tide goes out and the river all but vanishes. We clamber down the cliff and squelch our way through the claggy blue-grey mud. The children smother themselves with muddy warpaint and the rest of us treasure-hunt under the cliffs. They are spongy and unstable, a precarious wreckage of landslips, fossils, washed-out trees and flotsam, and we keep a nervous eye on the state of the river, even though the tide isn't due for hours. My friends tell me that when the local fishermen wade out at low water to put out their salmon basket-traps, they always wear two watches, just in case one stops. The Severn, even on such balmy days, remains a complex, unpredictable and moody river.

JULY 21 (1990)

Beech-mast so dense on the trees that it is obscuring the leaves, and making them look prematurely autumnal.

JULY 22

The new clutch of house martins hatch. Four neat eggshell halves lie under the nest, and the parents are flying back and forth with food every few minutes.

JULY 24

A spotted flycatcher haunts the garden. It is the perfect familiar for a garden in high summer, a creature of shaded trees and elegant forays over the lawn. They were favourites of the writer, Kenneth Allsop, in the garden of his Dorset mill house: 'Summer would not be the same without the flycatchers. When the air is still and the foliage hangs heavy in the afternoons with only a kaleidoscope of shifting coloured patterns of the butterflies upon the buddleias, the garden is made lively with their flashing plumage.'

Today our garden flycatcher, a contrary bird, sits *inside* the buddleia, eyeing the butterflies, but not on this occasion attempting to catch them.

JULY 25 *Chess Valley, Buckinghamshire Chilterns*

A great gathering of house martins by the river, some two hundred perched on telegraph wires and more hunting over the newly-cut grass fields and water meadows. They are mostly young birds, practising preening, and none too steady on their perches. I think to myself, rather unkindly, 'what easy pickings they would make for a hobby falcon' – forgetting momentarily how I scream and shout into the air whenever a hobby coasts over our martins' nest at home, and draws them up into rash mobbing flights.

A few minutes later I am leaning on a bridge and looking back down the river when the whole company of martins rises up in a tight mass. I wonder what on earth they are doing, and cannot believe that they are migrating so early. Then I see the hobby coasting just beneath them, a dark, glowering bird flying surprisingly slowly. I am relieved, for the sake of my conscience, that it hasn't taken my summons literally enough to begin chasing the martins.

JULY 26 *Pitstone Fen, Buckinghamshire*

Spectacular display of bee orchids, some with nine blooms on a single flower-spike. I become so blasé about them after a while that I mistake the front end of a puss moth larva on a willow leaf for a fallen blossom. This caterpillar looks extraordinary at any time, with its bloated pale green body and brown saddle. But when it is threatened it uncurls the bizarre 'face' which is normally hidden in the thorax, and which resembles a pink sea-urchin – or a bee-orchid flower, if that is what you are expecting.

JULY 27 *North Norfolk*

Long walk over the saltings at Stiffkey. Billows of sea lavender stretching all the way to the beach, broken with smaller flats and waves of emerald samphire, pea-green purslane and silver sea wormwood.

The weather brightens as we near the sea, and suddenly a mirage of Blakeney Point appears through the heat haze, floating just above the Point itself, so that mirage and real dunes merge into a shimmering sand cliff, like a scene from north Africa.

FLOWER OF THE MONTH

Lime or linden blossom is the sweetest and most penetrating of all our native tree flower-scents. In July it is sometimes possible to catch the scent of a single tree hundreds of yards away. You may *hear* the blossom from some way off, too, humming with the enormous company of nectar-gathering bees that swarms about them.

Limes are a mysterious and beautiful tribe at all times of the year. Most specimens are the planted common lime, *Tilia x vulgaris*, a hybrid between our two native species, the small- and large-leaved limes. (This hybrid occurs naturally in some woods on the limestone where both parents occur.)

Small-leaved lime, *Tilia cordata*, is a handsome tree with heart-shaped leaves and a smooth steel-grey bark, and was probably the commonest woodland tree in the south of England three thousand years ago. It still survives in woods in East Anglia, Hampshire, the Wye Valley, the Derbyshire Dales, Lincolnshire and the Lake District. The large-leaved is a rarer species, largely confined in the wild to woods in the Welsh border country and on the South Downs.

All limes have strong links with human communities, and have been coppiced, pollarded, carved for church orna-ments, planted as village green and boundary trees, and have served as hosts for mistletoe.

Lime blossom

AUGUST

Fledgling house martins

Edward Thomas once confessed that:

*I have found only two satisfying places in the world in August –
the Bodleian Library and a little reedy, willowy pond . . .
Through the willows I see the hot air quiver in crystal ripples like
the points of swords, and sometimes I see a crimson cyclist on a
gate. Thus is 'fantastic summer's heat' divine. For in August it is
right to be cool and at the same time enjoy the sight and perfume
of heat out of doors.* (*The Heart of England*, 1906)

The Bodleian Library is privileged territory, but in Oxford it
is possible to enjoy an atmosphere of sequestered scho-
larship in all manner of public places. One of these, the
University Botanic Garden, has a willowy pond as well,

which would have made it a feast for Thomas. It is the oldest of Britain's botanic gardens – and full of corners for august contemplation. The pond, decked out with bog and water plants, and haunted by dragonflies and accommodating birds, can be surveyed from the shade of a large weeping willow. There are invitingly bosky corners all over the garden – magnolias, pines, and swamp cypresses, service trees to lean against, thickets of scented viburnums and philadelphus to burrow in.

Edward Thomas was exactly right about the requirements for a perch in August heat. You need to be in a bower, gazing out. The shade of a tree, standing in grassland, is just the thing. So is an old gravestone, the underhang of a hedge by a wheatfield, a nest amongst ferns. A punt moored under a willow tree is almost perfect.

Cities are surprisingly good at providing such nooks. In London in high summer I have often searched out spots to rest up for a while, the urban equivalent of a five-bar gate. The walls at the edges of open-air car parks are a safe bet, perhaps because they overlook the nearest thing to open space in many parts of the city. One car park, in Marylebone, is often full of birds because it is also full of sentimental Londoners feeding them. In another, in Bloomsbury, feral cats snooze away summer afternoons on car roofs. There are temporary, short-lived, shady corners, too. A portable tub garden in Holborn. The community plots around Covent Garden. And a more orthodox green space, in an unexpected place: a little municipal enclave of pedestrian walkways, adventure playgrounds and tree-shaded benches in the middle of Camden, in sight of the fetchingly painted St Pancras gasometers.

AUGUST 2

The young martins are visible for the first time, a row of spiky Mohican crests bobbing at the nest entrance. When one of the parents arrives with food (every two minutes or so), all caution is thrown away and four froggy faces appear and squawk through the narrow hole.

AUGUST 6

The weather has turned cold and wet over the last couple of days, and the young martins have retreated to the depths of the nest. The parents vanish on long forays, and there were two-hour gaps between feeds this morning. How do they manage to bring back enough food for the young? Do they gather compacted balls of insects, as swifts do, making up in quantity for what they lack in frequency?

As they swoop back towards the nest entrance, drops of rainwater shower off their backs. I feel for them, caught out in the downpours, and fret about their chicks suffering from hypothermia. That afternoon I cycle off to see if I can find out where the adult birds forage. I have a vague image of some sheltered, communal feeding station, thronging with birds from all over the parish. But I find nothing of the kind, even after hours of searching. Instead, there are little packs of birds feeding wherever they can find shelter from the wind. I discover one single bird strafing backwards and forwards deep inside a canal lock, and another group skimming the tops and skirts of a lime tree, brushing against the leaves with their wings to dislodge insects.

A<small>UGUST</small>, F<small>IRST</small> W<small>EEK</small> *Cheshire*

The annual gooseberry shows in villages in Cheshire and west Yorkshire, last weekend of July to first weekend of August.

Growing prize gooseberries has been a passion in North Country mining villages – especially in mid-Cheshire – for nearly two centuries. The shows have been an integral part of a remarkable story of do-it-yourself plant breeding, which turned a small, humble wild berry into a sumptuous dessert fruit.

There is no record of the introduction of any cultivated varieties of gooseberry into Britain, nor even of cultivation itself before the sixteenth century. But by the mid-eighteenth century gooseberry growing had become a cult amongst cottagers in the industrial north and Midlands. By the beginning of the twentieth century as many as two thousand varieties (often named after national heroes, battles, politicians) were in circulation. All had their origins in the wild bushes, which were taken into tiny gardens and backyards and encouraged to crossbreed and set seed. Seedlings that produced promising berries would be propagated by cuttings.

One of the great spurs to continued improvement in variety and size were the gooseberry shows, in which individual berries of the same colour were matched against one another. These still continue in villages such as Goostrey, Peover, Swettenham and Marton in Cheshire, and Egton Bridge in Yorkshire, and the techniques and rituals have barely changed.

The gooseberry plants (known locally as 'trees' rather than bushes) are grown in low frames (pens) and protected by drapes and nets against all kinds of damage. The picking of the ripe berries for show is done in the presence of a witness,

Magdalen backwater with pollard willow

usually another competitor, and the fruits are sealed into padded boxes. The next day they are taken out with great care (to be ready for showing they must be close to bursting) and weighed, using the archaic Troy system of weights.

Despite fierce competition, gooseberry growing is a very sociable business, and cuttings from new varieties are freely exchanged amongst enthusiasts. And the berries themselves remain one of the most delectable of fruits. Even at their most monstrous (some can be as big as duck eggs) they have a sweetness and succulence and range of flavours absent from ordinary stewing gooseberries.

AUGUST 8

Temperatures return to above 30°C (86°F), and it is only tolerable to sit outside in the shade. In spite of the heat, a robin sings a continuous, touchingly introspective sub-song in the lilac bush just behind me. I sit, reflecting on the mellow harmonies of this season, and watching a flightless female moth crawling laboriously across the lawn, just inches from my feet. With barely a pause in its song the robin swoops down and swallows it whole.

AUGUST 14 (1970) *Western Highlands*

Climbing Beinn Eighe in Ross and Cromarty. Above fifteen hundred feet a real Alpine landscape opens up, with cowberry and a few pink-flowered sprigs of our native wild azalea. The terraced, near-vertical faces of the quartz and sandstone rocks give the whole landscape a two-dimensional look. This is peregrine falcon country, and we are not disappointed.

The pair that appear over the cliffs are my very first. We hear them before seeing them, a sound like the creaking of a rusty gate as they soar above us. I am amazed at their sheer bulk, and then begin to notice small details – the dense muscle at the forward edge of their wings, the way these are held in a slight downward tilt as they glide.

AUGUST 10 *The Chess Valley, Buckinghamshire Chilterns*

A juvenile kestrel, not yet up to taking larger prey, hunts grasshoppers or beetles, by perching on a telegraph wire and plunging onto the pasture below.

AUGUST 15 *Selborne, Hampshire*

Some two hundred mixed martins and swallows playing and feeding round the Hanger, especially under the lip of the topmost tier of trees, where insects are sucked off by the wind's downdraught.

AUGUST 16

The intense heat has pushed the local woodlands into a kind of premature autumn. The bracken tips are tinged with brown, the first blackberries are ripe, and rowan trees are laden with uneaten fruit. Dragonflies haunt the rides, but nothing else stirs. A sparrowhawk hurtles across a young chestnut plantation and dog-legs down a ride – a blur of rust and gunmetal grey. But there is not a single small bird in sight. Like us, they lie up in the heat. They only put themselves at real risk if they panic and make a break for it.

AUGUST 17

The martin chicks have been active and excited for the past couple of days, bobbing up and down in the nest, squabbling and stretching their wings. The ones at the entrance keep disappearing backwards, and the others wriggle forward for their turn. Sometimes I'm sure they stand on each other. They look like young otters, perched upright at the hole. They must be very close to flying.

Today the largest chick begins to hang out of the nest, right up to its chest. It already has an almost full adult plumage. Its bristly crest has been replaced by a smooth, sooty cap and a silky white front. It peers around as usual – up at its own shadow, down at the spiders spinning webs round the base of the nest, out at passers-by and cars, and especially at the white butterflies dithering past the nest. It follows their progress towards the roof until its head is screwed round at at almost a hundred and eighty degrees. Then, suddenly a chick again, its beak gapes involuntarily. It is dreaming of food.

Now the parents are teasing the chicks, flying up as if to feed them, then darting away. They cling to the wall very close to the nest and weave their heads at the youngsters like snake charmers. One youngster seems almost on the point of popping out when they all cower back in the nest at the sight of a yellow British Telecom van.

About lunchtime the biggest chick comes to the nest hole again, stretches its neck forward with a curious exultant churring note, and pops out like a champagne cork. The next is out a few minutes later and they are soon both flying as airily as their parents, dashing back and forth to the nest entrance and chivvying the remaining youngsters.

AUGUST, MIDDLE WEEK *South Downs Way, Sussex*

A blazing hot and clear day, but with a breeze off the sea. The remnants of chalk grassland that line the track are still thick with downland flowers – thyme, marjoram, harebells and a scatter of the dark blue, globular flowers of rampion. There are majestic views of the Wealden woodland to the north, and the sweeps of downland rolling down to the sea. In the arable plains on the foothills and flat valley land, the combine harvesters are edging forward in dust-wreathed echelons, a triumphant and spectacular procession that seems, on this golden day at least, to justify our profligacy with corn. I am reminded of Thomas Traherne's seventeenth-century meditation:

> *The orient and immortal wheat, which never should be reaped, nor was ever sown. I thought it had stood from everlasting to everlasting.*

AUGUST 19

'Ant-rising day' on our lawn. All the flying ants over quite a large area leave their nests for mating on the same day. The few queens and the many smaller males fly up together, and for a while the air is full of the glitter of their wings against the sun, like a slow shower of tinsel. About twenty minutes later the females return to earth, bite off their wings and go underground to lay their eggs – if they succeed in escaping the bands of marauding red ants that also gather for the feast.

It is the one and only time they ever take to the air. I ponder again the dramatic, arcane world of insect life, seemingly so alien to our own.

But later a red admiral butterfly settles on my arm and, relaxing under its calming presence, I am able to feel every movement of its tongue as it samples the salt perspiration on my skin.

AUGUST 23 *Chess Valley, Buckinghamshire Chilterns*

Many small flocks of martins passing through. The birds in one group, about a hundred strong, drop out of the sky and, in orderly formation, begin skimming the surface of a riverside pool. Are they drinking, or catching flies? They repeat the manoeuvre three times, keeping quite high formation above the water both before and after their dives, then all fly off towards the north again at a great height.

Later, close to home, I meet a loose flock of about fifty birds coasting leisurely across the stubble fields from the south. They have an easy, dipping but purposeful flight, as if they are returning to the nest colony after a long journey, and I am struck with the fancy that they may have been to the seaside for the day.

AUGUST 26 *Hickling Broad, Norfolk*

Variations on a harvest theme: a pair of marsh harriers in their full aerial food-passing display, somersaulting and diving with a small bundle of prey (probably a vole) – directly above an impressive new piece of farm machinery that is rolling up straw into circular bales and dropping them about the field.

AUGUST 27 *Walberswick, Suffolk*

Swimming and sun-bathing on the shingle beach, and rolling over from time to time to watch the migratory waders stopping off to feed on the pools just inland from the shingle. There are trickles of knot, ringed plover, and curlew sandpiper in with the ubiquitous dunlin. Then become aware of something unfamiliar just a few yards from our noses: a small ruff-like bird, narrow-necked and delicate, that picks up its long legs like a water-rail when it walks. A buff-breasted sandpiper, a rare vagrant from North America.

FLOWER OF THE MONTH

Buddleia, the butterfly bush, has been in Britain for less than a century, yet it is already one of the commonest plants in urban Britain, cropping up in seemingly soilless stretches of wasteland, on ruined walls, even growing out of chimneys. It is in flower from early July in some warm spots, but August is its best month.

Buddleia's natural home is rocky scree in the western Chinese foothills, and it was from here that specimens were sent back to England. Once established as a garden shrub it began to spread in the wild, and found the clutter of the urban fringe a passable substitute for its original home. Above all habitats, it loves the stony wastes of the railway system, and many stretches of line are so thickly fringed with bushes that they have become a kind of oriental scrubland.

It is a favourite with butterflies, and sometimes, when a train stops at a signal in August, dozens may be visible flitting about the bushes only a few feet from the carriage window.

SEPTEMBER

London birds

Late summer to early autumn is the best time for rambling in the city. It is the built-up area's equivalent of spring, when luxuriant growth finally outstrips municipal tidiness, and a pleasantly scruffy off-green bloom seems to spread over any unguarded surface. I once glimpsed a gang of noisy pheasants taking refuge in the undergrowth of a Hackney rubbish tip on the first day of the shooting season (October 1), and thought it one of the most cheering things I had ever seen in London.

I did a true hike round London, a two-day thirty-mile ramble chiefly along the ring of marginal land where the inner city frays into the industrial and residential belts. But I began in central London, in St James's Park. This is about as far from the urban wild as you can get, the haunt of

bird-watching civil servants and one of the biggest assort-
ments of semi-tame waterbirds. Yet, even here, you can
glimpse the opportunism that is the basic survival technique
of all urban wildlife. In these Westminster pleasure grounds
city creatures adjust to the human life styles of their chosen
niche with a rather special panache. They are quarrelsome
and ingratiating, and ostentatious supporters of the enterprise culture. That day there were pigeons and sparrows
feeding *inside* one favoured human's parcel of scraps. Crows,
against their more usual solitary nature, were loafing
around in packs. One, with a stick in its beak, seemed to be
digging for worms.

Out on St James's lake there were a few wilder birds –
great crested grebes, still in their raffish chestnut breeding
plumage, and a scatter of house martins skimming low over
the surface. I followed the martins across Belgravia, and
their numbers increased as I got closer to Hyde Park and their
celebrated nesting site on the French Embassy.

House martins feed entirely on airborne insects and had to
quit Central London altogether in the 1880s, when air
pollution wiped out their food supply. They began trickling
back in the late 1960s, and now nest in half a dozen sites
within a couple of miles of Trafalgar Square. This communal
eyrie, eighty feet or so above Knightsbridge, must be one of
the most strangely situated and safest in the country. The
Embassy eaves have rows of indentations, in each of which is
an ornamental four-lobed stone rosette. The martins build
inside the cavities, with their nests propped up on the lobes.

I wondered how, amidst all the residential opportunities
in the city, they had lit upon this well-nigh perfect site. But I
have seen them prospecting around the consulate and quan-
go buildings in Belgrave Square, and sometimes swarming
round the eaves of the Ministry of Defence, and like to think
they have a connoisseur's eye for secure properties. As I

watched them flitting over the traffic to hunt for aphids in Hyde Park – canny, adaptable birds, tolerant of human company without surrendering a jot of wildness – they seemed to be an apt symbol of London's wildlife, and a mascot for urban ramblers, too.

There wasn't much else about in the Park. But in Notting Hill Gate things began to look up. Here wild plants have begun to ease their way into street life. In Ladbroke Grove, wherever there is room for people to stop and chat, feed the pigeons, spill their shopping, the cracks in the pavement bristle with seedlings of sweet corn, wheat, millet, tomatoes and the occasional mung bean. Up by the jumble of gasworks and railway sidings near the Harrow Road, herbaceous thickets shoot out of the gutters and even the chimneys.

Ahead were the cryptic shrubberies of Kensal Green, good fox country. I didn't spot one that day. But, one June, passing the cemetery in a slow train, I saw a vixen and three cubs basking on the embankment in the sunshine. Foxes live a largely unmolested but vagrant existence in London, sleeping rough and raiding dustbins rather than chicken runs. But this doesn't guarantee them a carefree life. One vet, who has done postmortems on London foxes, has found they have a tendency to suffer from the same diet-based disorders as their unwitting hosts, especially, these days, hardening of the arteries.

Making-do is an essential tactic in urban ecology. The Grand Union canal, which winds off east from Kensal Green under the swooping shadow of the Westway, does service as London's nearest equivalent to a *small* river. Moorhens perch on floating tyres. Riverside flowers – marsh woundwort, skullcap, wild angelica and great sheaves of sweet flag – crowd along the edge of the towpath.

I stayed on the towpath and passed through Little Venice, where the houseboats sport deck-top gardens and ship's cats. It is uncanny how wildlife – plants especially – marks out the city's social and cultural divisions so accurately. In Regent's Park, Paddington's rowdy exotics give way to dappled shrubberies. The water becomes as clear as a rural stream. There are bankside spikes of purple loosestrife, the flower which Millais used to ornament the edge of the stream in his painting of Ophelia's drowning. Bullfinches, white rumps flashing, darted between the hawthorns. I spotted a kestrel planing into an ash tree, and would have spent a while watching it, if I hadn't become aware of a boy's face peering at me through the bushes, like a Jack-in-the-Green. I've no idea if he thought he was invisible, but it was one of the more intriguing glimpses of feral behaviour of the day.

It was another kestrel that was my last sighting of the day, as I sat on a lock gate and watched the sun go down by the bistros and craft shops of Camden Lock. It banked out of the sunset and away over the evening traffic jam building up in Camden High Street. City kestrels have lives far removed from those of their soaring downland cousins. They are streetwise, inventive, snatching sparrows from the rooftops and nesting in high-rise style, from gasometers to tower-blocks.

The next day I went on a few miles to the clutter of wharves, marshalling yards and small factories round Lea Bridge, and set off across what was once Hackney Marsh. It is now one of the biggest football pitches in the world, but though it has been drained and manicured seemingly to the point of sterilisation, the spirit of the old swamp hasn't been entirely banished. A kestrel hunched on a pylon. Canada geese straggled in from Walthamstow reservoirs to the north. A heron loped by. Then, quite suddenly, the air was alive with swooping black and white birds. It was the house martins again. A flock of some two hundred, migrating casually south, had materialised from nowhere and begun hawking for flies over the field. A few – they are innately playful birds – began slaloming through the goalposts.

I took off south, too, down the new Hackney Cut. This is an ordinary canal walk for the first few miles, and I had the company of big, blue-and-black-striped emperor dragon-flies, which were darting above the polystyrene flotsam. But by Stratford Marsh it had turned into a jungle track. Festoons of Russian vine covered the factory fences and half blocked the towpath. There were drifts of dwarf elder and michael-mas daisy. In places the towpath burrowed under long complexes of railway bridges, and for hundreds of claus-trophobic yards I was walking in semi-darkness on a tow-path only a couple of feet wide.

But then, opposite a breaker's yard where rows of dis-carded phone boxes had been lined up along the bank, I heard the thin, metallic skirl of a black redstart, the bird above all others I had hoped to see. Black redstarts, rather like dusky robins with rufous tails, haunt rocky hillsides and stone-built villages throughout mainland Europe, and be-gan finding the bombed-out moraine of Inner London a passable substitute during the war. Since then they have nested in Woolwich Arsenal, Broad Street Station, the fire-places of bombed-out buildings in the Temple, East End windowsills and innumerable gasworks.

I walked on south, through Poplar, and then turned west along the East India Dock Road towards the piazzas and design studios of the new Dockland. Paradoxically, there is not much access to water here. Even the Thames has been straightened up and hemmed in. I spotted a grey wagtail bobbing on the shingle edges of the Shadwell watersports basin, but that is one of the few places here where you can even catch a glimpse of the capital's river.

But Shadwell, at least, has a house martin colony, under

the balconies of a block of 1930s' flats. These are the very last buildings before the vast development site by the Shadwell basin. I had seen the birds earlier in the year gathering mud for nesting out of the ruts cut up by the bulldozers, and this afternoon they were hawking for flies over the weed-strewn spoil tips, past the Indian corner shop and over the patch of grass and staked trees that passes for the local park. But for the most part they feed where they can over the so-far undeveloped buddleia patches and churchyards.

Buddleia growing on a London wall

Even these are vanishing fast. The last time I had seen the little churchyard in Scandrett Street, it had been a muddle of old tombs, long grass and wildflowers, a green retreat for children and loungers, as well as an oasis for feeding martins. Now some tidy-minded planners have moved the gravestones up to the wall, shorn the grass and ringed it with beds full of funereal evergreens. As I walked up Wapping High Street towards it, I could see that a photographic team were working near the railings, taking stills of a bright scarlet postbox over which tumbled a spray of wild hops. I was trying to remember whether the box had been so rustically adorned when I was last here, when one of the crew folded up the cardboard fake and packed it away in the car. This is the kind of fate often suffered by the wilder fringes of 'heritage' London.

But further along Wapping High Street I spotted a black redstart at last, exploring the remains of a Port of London Authority building, now sandwiched between new flats and a garden centre. Soon it was joined by a female, and the two dark-grey waifs flitted about the sooty stonework, with that slight, evocative call echoing between the walls.

I was three miles short of St James's by the time dusk fell. The starling flocks that roost in the Park were massing overhead, and yet more groups of martins were grabbing their last feed of the day over the heads of Wapping's commuters, and I felt that the circuit was more or less complete.

SEPTEMBER 1

There has been a rapid change to fresher weather over the past forty-eight hours, and birds have started to reappear. I sit in the garden in the early evening, and watch the fly-past. Greenfinches are dapping for berries on the elder bush. A straggling band of long-tailed tits dart furtively into the willow tree, as if they are trying to fly on tiptoe. A late, lone swift coasts easily towards the east, and just a minute later a female sparrowhawk glides low across the garden in the opposite direction, climbing fast towards the big plane tree. She is on a hunting foray, and causes havoc amongst the starlings that are massing for their evening roost. They tumble out of the sky in mock swoons.

SEPTEMBER 5 *Tring Reservoirs, Hertfordshire*

The heat has produced an extraordinary growth of a blue-green algae (known locally as 'water-net') which resembles a tangle of string-bags. It has attracted an immense number of freshwater crustaceans, and wagtails and sandpipers are browsing across the surface, sinking slightly each time they take a step on the rubbery green matting.

SEPTEMBER 6

The martins are still returning to roost in the nest. Just after 11 p.m. I shine a torch through one of the holes which are beginning to appear in the caked mud shell, and see the slightly quivering underside of one bird, and knobbly bits of feet and vents. But I keep the beam on too long, and one martin squirms towards the nest entrance, composes itself, and peers disgruntledly towards me. It is upside down, and I feel a pang of guilt at disturbing it during roosting hours.

SEPTEMBER 12

A hobby falcon soars leisurely over the house late in the afternoon. It has materialised out of the pall of smoke over a late stubble fire to the north, hunting, I imagine, for fleeing insects – or perhaps for the martins and swallows that are drawn to the edge of these fires after the same prey.

It is an awesomely accomplished flier, making distance with relaxed, rather elbowy beats, coasting briefly on long rapier wings held out flat, then twisting and banking in an almost vertical plane, so that I glimpse its rufous leg feathers.

I often see hobbies over the garden at this time of year, when their own young are fledged and they take to a more roving life. But these flights out of the stubble fields are a movable feast, and when there is an early harvest I have sometimes seen them as early as the first week in August.

SEPTEMBER 20

The last mowing of the verges, a profitable time for twen-tieth-century archaeologists, or anyone curious about the changing accoutrements of rural life. The verge and its accompanying ditch are the countryside's common dump-ing ground, both for those who work there and those who pass through. The cartoonist Posy Simmonds once drew up a field-guide to the more recent deposits:

> *The lane banks are gay with* DROPFOIL, GUMBANE *and* YELLOW CORN COCKLE, *and in lay-by nooks, colonies of* BUFF-TIPPED LUNG BUTTS. *Here also we find the first* GOBLINS FINGERSTALLS *peering through the grasses, waxy gold or translucent pink . . .*

The objects that cluster randomly together often have the cryptic fascination of clues in an old-fashioned murder mys-tery. In one short stretch of verge I once found an unused pack of horse vaccine ampoules, the carcass of an owl and, from some earlier period of litter spreading, an earthenware bottle from a 'Botanic Brewery'.

Deeper still the verge becomes a time capsule. Ronald Blythe, who once dug up an eighteenth-century stained-glass window and the remains of a Spitfire instrument panel in his Suffolk garden, has written:

If families have lived for four or more centuries on a spot where the dustman has only been calling since about 1947, and which lies along the edge of a road which men have been travelling since long before Gregory I was diplomatically designating the inhabitants not Angles but angels, it is obvious that one's whole life revolves just a few spade lengths from a vast range of artefacts.

SEPTEMBER 23

An Indian summer, with a flat, pearly sky. At five o'clock in the afternoon a small flight of noctule bats appears high over the town, about a quarter of a mile away. I think they are swifts at first, from their furious darting and plunging flight, and then snipe. They are flying at about two hundred feet, on migration perhaps, and occasionally seem to be dive-bombing each other.

SEPTEMBER 30 *New Forest*

A fine autumn day, with a breeze off the sea, and the damp valleys scented with bog myrtle. On a heath near Bolder-wood I am gazing out towards the south when I see a pert, dusky-plumaged warbler darting about between the gorse clumps. It flicks its tail up on landing and, even from a distance, I can make out its flanks shining the colour of heather flowers in the sun. It is a Dartford warbler, my first ever. Through binoculars I can see its brilliant red eyes and steel-grey back – and one other remarkable thing: the air between us is full of strings of transparent gossamer, and the warbler is feasting on money spiders, dangled out of the sky.

FLOWERS OF THE MONTH

A London flora

London doesn't possess much in the way of a truly native flora. London rocket, which acquired its name from shooting spectacularly through the rubble after the Great Fire of 1666, vanished in the nineteenth century. London Pride is now better known as a real ale than an occasional escape from suburban rockeries. The only truly wild species openly to commemorate the capital is London ragwort, a drab hybrid between two species whose parentage – *Senecio squalidus* out of *S. viscosus* – sounds like a pedigree from Mayhew's account of the Victorian underworld.

Perhaps rose-bay willow herb, in flower from July to early October, is London's true floral mascot. It was already becoming a familiar urban weed early in the century, but the fires and devastation of the Blitz gave its airborne seeds unprecedented opportunities to spread, and from the summer of 1940 it began to cover the ruins of the City and East End with a purple carpet. It still prospers on waste patches throughout the capital, even those only left vacant for a few years.

The most successful urban wildflowers are all opportunists and vagrants, making do with whatever pockets of open

ground they can find. In big cities like London, they are also
cosmopolitan, and the origins of many in other parts of the
globe show up in their collective tendency to flower late in
the year. September and even October are their showiest
months.

Like all urban wildlife they also reflect London's social and
economic history. Naturalised garden plants, for example,
are one of the stocks-in-trade of London's flora. The drifts of
American golden rod and michaelmas daisy that now line
the edges of railway tracks and National Car Parks mostly
date from after the war, when their rather gross luxuriance
went out of fashion in small gardens. The awesome giant
hogweed (it grows ten feet tall and in July has flower heads
the size of car wheels) was thrown out rather earlier. The
best colonies are in the western suburbs, but there are
pockets in Regent's Park, and even in Buckingham Palace
Gardens.

There are relics of old physic gardens, too. The livid
purple-veined flowers of henbane, source of one of Dr
Crippen's poisons, have cropped up in the car park of the
Festival Hall. Deadly nightshade grew till quite recently in
the grounds of Guy's Hospital, where it may once have been
cultivated as a sedative. Dormant seeds from old herb gardens may also be responsible for the thornapples (a Peruvian
plant resembling an herbaceous conker) that tend to appear
in London gardens after hot summers. But why the
Mediterranean shrub bladder senna, which was once grown
as a cheap laxative, should be so concentrated round railway
sidings in the East End is one of London's more teasing
botanical mysteries. Its swollen seed pods are evident in
September.

In the north and east of London you can sometimes find
industrial and commercial stowaways. The most famous is
the colony of prairie tumbleweed that survives (with chang-

ing fortunes) on the ash tips at the Ford works in Dagenham. The seeds came to Britain in packing cases of parts from the USA. Food species normally arrive in a more straightforward fashion, and are certainly more widespread. Tomato plants grow on most waste patches and rubbish tips. So do the commoner spices and herbs – fennel, coriander, poppies – anywhere that seeds might be spilt from a jar. More exotic food plants, such as cumin, gram and watermelon have all increased as London's ethnic populations have grown, but they tend to do best in the composted warmth of the big local authority refuse tips. But how the peanut bush which grew near Shepperton managed to sprout and survive in our climate is another puzzle.

Yet what makes the London flora so intriguing is not just what turns up, but the where-and-how of it. The whole company makes up an extraordinary saga of opportunism and adaptation. Bright blue lobelias in the pavement cracks, seeded from second-floor window boxes. Ferns in the basements, revelling in the shade. (In Belgrave Square I have seen a male fern straining against the glass insert of a manhole cover). Bird-seed species, like canary grass, growing in the minimal soils at the foot of street trees. And one ubiquitous late-flowering species, in doorstep tubs, at the foot of hoardings, even growing from the now less frequently swept gutters. *Galinsoga parviflora* is a rather drab and drooping daisy from Peru. It was first noticed growing wild in Richmond in the 1890s, presumably escaped from nearby Kew Gardens, and became known locally as Kew-weed. Then its airborne seeds began wafting over less elegant postal districts, and a more general and down-to-earth name was needed. *Galinsoga* was too much of a mouthful, so with a nice touch of irony it was bowdlerised into Gallant Soldiers.

117

OCTOBER

Wild Service berries

The best month for picking wild crops of all kinds. Some of the commoner fruits may be past their best, but there is no moment of the year when there is a greater variety. It is a time for wayside nibbling, browsing and sampling, what the 1930s' fruit gourmet, Edward Bunyard, called 'ambulant consumption'.

Hazelnuts are at their best, though not many will remain on the bushes. Try searching inside the bush where the nuts may have been sheltered from wind and squirrels.

The first *sweet chestnuts* will be coming down. There is no need to roast them; the bigger ones are perfectly edible raw, if a little dry.

Field mushrooms, *parasols* and *ceps* can also be nibbled raw in small quantities, though should be checked for grubs first by twisting the stem free. (Insects nearly always gain access through the stem, and leave their telltale burrowing channels.)

Don't spurn the *blackberry*. Even quite late in October there will be perfectly acceptable specimens about, though not as large and luscious as the early berries. Try searching out odd varieties and flavours. There are four hundred different micro-species in Britain, and many of them have subtle after-tastes, of apple, plum, and grape.

And don't forget the *dewberry*, the blackberry's closest relative, easily distinguished by its fewer segments covered with fine bloom. Dewberries are so juicy that they often burst as you pluck them from the bush. A way of avoiding this is to snip off the last inch of the stalk and eat them like cocktail cherries.

Other fruits worth eating straight off the tree or bush are:

Late *raspberries* in shady corners. These are so often entangled with brambles that it looks as if two fruits are growing on the same bush.

Rowanberries, for those with a taste for bitter things.

The first fully reddened *haws*, with a texture like under-ripe avocados.

Crab and *wilding apples*. Trees with intriguingly flavoured fruits can spring from discarded apple cores, and these have been the origin of many famous cultivated varieties, such as Granny Smith, Lane's Prince Albert and Discovery.

After the first frosts all fruits become softer and sweeter. *Wild plums* (bullaces, damsons, etc) become quite delectable, and even the forbiddingly tart *sloe* can just about be endured raw after a few freezing days.

The most intriguing of wild fruits made palatable by frosts is the *serviceberry*. Sadly this grows on what is one of the most local and least known of all our native trees. The wild service tree is a relative of the whitebeam and rowan. It occurs sparsely right across England and Wales, but only on hard limestone soils (in the west) and stiff clays. Spreading mostly by suckers, it is also restricted to long-established woodland, and to hedgerows derived from ancient woods. The fruits, which are round or pear-shaped and the size of small cherries, are hard and sour at first, but as autumn progresses they 'blet' and turn soft, brown and sweet. The taste is unlike anything else which grows wild in this country, with hints of apricot, sultana, tamarind and prune.

Remains of the berries have been found in a number of archaeological sites, and they must have been a boon when other sources of sugar were in short supply. In areas where the tree was relatively widespread, the fruits continued to be a popular dessert right up to the beginning of this century. In the Kentish Weald they were gathered before they had bletted and were strung up in clusters round a stick, which was hung up indoors, often by the hearth. The individual serviceberries were picked off and eaten like sweets as they ripened.

In a good year the harvest could be huge (one surviving tree in the Weald with a fourteen-foot girth can produce two tons of berries) and the surplus was often fermented into a beer. It's possible that a southern English name for the berries, *Chequers*, may derive from this use in brewing – a Chequers pub specialising in serviceberry beer giving its name to the fruit.

OCTOBER 2 *Ashridge Park, Chilterns*

The fallen beeches have the first good show of fungi. One trunk has more than a dozen species, including the ethereal beech tuft, whose pallid, translucent caps melt like candle-wax as they age, and edible oyster mushrooms with caps the colour of slate.

OCTOBER 3

Sudden change to cooler weather, with strong blustery winds. As if to mark the change of season, the neighbour's tortoise reappears in our garden, looking for a place to hibernate. It has been at its rightful address all summer and carries '28 Poplar Drive' painted in red and silver on a newly-oiled shell. But as it has every winter for some years now, it finds a gap in the fence, plods into our garden and laboriously buries itself in our compost heap.

OCTOBER 4

Our own martins seem to have departed, and are no longer roosting in the nest. But at about 9.30 this morning a swarm of some thirty martlets, probably the neighbourhood youngsters, descend on the house. They are fascinated by the sight of a solitary, empty nest, and swoop about for more than an hour. They are meant to be practising for the serious business of nest-prospecting next spring, but their outing erupts into a boisterous game. They struggle to get into the nest, and two succeed. More – I count eight at one point – cling to the outside trying to pull the squatters out. But they are relishing playing at adults and won't be budged. They begin hurling out the nest lining, exactly as if it were May and they were beginning to set up house themselves.

The remainder rush up and down the road, rising in small waves of four or five under any promising eaves, skimming almost through my hair at times, resting up on roofs and wires. Then some discover the guttering above the nest. They stand on the roof, jump in, march backwards and forwards along it, and jump back on the roof again. It is an hilarious performance, and other birds are gathering to watch, sparrows staring at this mass invasion of their gutter, a blue tit wobbling in amazement on the telegraph wire.

OCTOBER 8 *The Norfolk Broads*

An off-season cruise in classic Norfolk weather, gusty winds, sheets of rain curling in over the flat land and scurrying away again.

The Broads have an indomitable air of cheeriness that I am sure is partly due to their resemblance to an aquatic village fête. There are solemn herons in the gardens of the home-built shacks and bungalows, so still and unflappable they are often mistaken for garden ornaments. Ingratiating grebes and coots bob close to the boat's wake, heads tilted in the hope of tit-bits. Guelder rose and wild hop sprawl from the edges of the alder scrub over fences of waterside pubs. And, at dusk, the evening flight of the ducks is followed smartly by the night-time crawl of the Mississippi-style paddle-boats.

Many of the boats are travelling above the legal speed limit, and remorselessly eroding the bank vegetation with their washes. The water itself is notoriously polluted from farm fertilisers and sewage. But the Broads are by no means a lost cause. We cruise briefly round one beautiful broad at South Walsham, where mooring and fishing are banned, and the edge vegetation is a dappled mix of reed and bulrush, visibly advancing out into the water. We follow a nature trail at Ranworth, a wooden causeway that passes from open broad to oak woodland via all the stages of succession by which one turns into the other.

It is chastening to remember that the Broads are the remains of peat-mines dug in the medieval period, and I find myself wondering what went wrong. Why were these mines abandoned and allowed to flood in the fourteenth century? Why did people, wise in the ways of managing renewable resources, abandon their usual modest style of harvesting peat (stripping surface layers and allowing the peat time to form again) and dig these deep and vulnerable pits down to the water table? Were they trying to meet an abnormal demand, after better-burning turves, or just plain greedy? Whatever the reason it is salutary to remember that the much-loved Broads, now given the same kind of protection as a national park, were formed as the result of a reckless adventure in land management and later abandoned. These days, they probably wouldn't even get planning permission.

Sailing on Norfolk Broads

OCTOBER 27 *The High Chilterns*

A spectacular autumn day in the hills. Walking in the rich chalk scrub-land near Ellesborough. Maple, cherry, spindle, and dogwood leaves are a kaleidoscope of vermilion, crimson, chestnut and lemon yellow, and the air is very sharp and clear. But in the deep combe, where a box wood grows, there is a humid, rainforest feel; a tunnel of deep shade under the tangled, iron-hard trunks, and that sour, evocative smell of the box leaves, evergreen against the bronze beeches beyond.

OCTOBER 30

All the neighbourhood martins are gone now, and the sky seems empty without them. But always at the end of October, or sometimes in early November, there is a reminder of them – a flock of late migrants passing through from the north, coasting about the autumn fields and meadows, bound for Africa.

Our own martins will already be foraging thousands of feet up in the skies above the Equator, sleeping on the wing. In less than fifteen weeks they will begin flying north again, and among them – if they have survived the ordeals of the journeys – will be a family of birds with a precise memory of the directions to the ideal home. Over the Channel, follow the chalk ridge north-east, turn right at the reservoirs, through the long market town almost to its end, and look for a house with a mud-spattered east-facing wall above a bed of sprawling rose-bushes . . .

FLOWER OF THE MONTH

Meadow saffron, *Colchicum autumnale*, which looks like a crocus and is really a lily, is an altogether contrary plant. Its six satin-sheened mauve petals appear months after its leaves have died away, giving it an appearance so starkly naked that this is remarked on in almost every local name, from Yorkshire ('naked ladies') to southern France (*cul tout nu*). It used to be found in hay meadows, yet it can be fatally poisonous to cattle, and contains a potent toxin (colchicine) which causes plant cells to mutate and is still a specific treatment for gout. When the Elizabethan herbalists first saw meadow saffron (its accepted English name, though it is not related to the saffron crocus either) they noted down its sites in untypical detail. William Turner made the first written record in 1551, and reported that it grew more 'in the west cuntre besyde Bath'. Fifty years later John Gerard gave such exact directions that you could still walk to the spot:

> *Purple English Meadow Saffron . . . in Kingstroppe medow neere unto a Watermill as you go from Northampton to Homeby House, upon the right hand of the way, and likewise in great plenty in Nobottle wood two miles from the said towne of Northampton . . .*

Like Turner he had also seen it – or heard about it – in the Mendips, 'in great abundance, as about Vilford and Bathe, as also in the medowes neere to a small village in the West part of England, called Shepton Mallet'.

The meadows near Northampton and round Bath have long been ploughed up, but meadow saffron still survives in the Mendips. I have found it in the local ashwoods, and can only say of my first encounter with it in this setting that the flowers seemed to *swim* into view. They were growing in a small dappled clearing, and were lying flat, their long pallid stalks twisted among the ground vegetation with the rosy-mauve flowers wide open. It was as if they had been squirted out of the ground and the thin shanks had not been strong enough to support their own weight. There were more clumps by the side of tracks, all of them in the same disarray. I hadn't seen the plant looking like this before, and wondered if the strong winds of the previous few days had had something to do with it. Or perhaps the darkness of a coppice that had not been cut for half a century had made them race up too ambitiously for the light. They had the look of almost anything but flowers; I was reminded of toothpaste at first, then seaweed, then of a kind of flowering toadstool.

In open meadowland *Colchicum* grows shorter, fatter and brighter. But this is a declining habitat, and was always problematic for farmers because of the poisonousness of meadow saffron's leaves. It could only really be tolerated where fields were 'shut up' for hay in the spring, cut in July after the leaves had died down and grazed for the short period before the flowers appeared. This was how many lowland meadows were managed anyway. (Though a farmer with *Colchicum* on his land might forgo winter grazing, and make do with selling a proportion of the corms as a cash crop for the pharmaceutical industry. In the last war, when overseas supplies were cut off, the Ministry of Health harvested the corms for colchicine all over Britain.) Few such meadows survive, and *Colchicum*'s heartland has now shrunk to a scatter of woods, old orchards, churchyards and rough grassland stretching along the border country between the Mendips and Wyre Forest.

NOVEMBER

Brent geese flying over saltmarshes

Trailing birds through the mist, one of the essential, tantalis-ing, pleasures of the month. Bands of redwings and fieldfares shuttle through the hawthorns just ahead of me, a clacking, rustling presence always just beyond visibility. Herons, moorhens, grey wagtails, and shapes too vague to identify, materialise briefly then dissolve again in the murk. A sparrowhawk glides across, followed smartly by a small jinking falcon. It is probably just a kestrel, made to look squat and dark by the mist. But this is the season for apparitions and fantasies, and I indulge myself in the possibility of a merlin. I remember childhood bird-watching always seem-ing to be just like this – full of romantic hopefulness and astonishment at the crossing of paths with wanderers from another country.

November 7

Mixed-season weather in the Chilterns. The sun shining palely on the mist in the hillside woods makes them look as if they are covered with hoar frost. The wild cherries and field maples are still draped with crimson and gold leaves, and a balmy breeze is blowing from the south-west.

Only two days later it is warm with high, summery cloud. Pied wagtails are feeding in the winter wheat, winter thrush flocks in the old man's beard. One final, solitary house martin dips and dives through the gnat clouds, looking 'brisk' as Gilbert White would have said. In the last century Richard Jefferies used to note spells like this a little earlier, in October:

> *I do not know of any other period of the year which exhibits so remarkable an assemblage of the representative features of the four quarters: an artist might design an emblematic study upon it, say for a tessellated pavement. (Wild Life in a Southern County, 1879)*

November 12

A fine, sharp autumn morning. A blackbird sips dew out of the concave cap of a toadstool on the lawn.

A great crop of shaggy parasol mushrooms has sprung up in Hardings Wood, ranged in fairy rings round some of the holly bushes. I take a handful back for supper, and they are so delectable that I fix up an outdoor lunch in the wood for the following Sunday, when we will be having our first workday of the winter, doing path-clearance and thinnings.

We take olive oil and wine down to the wood in the back of the pick-up truck, and fry the parasols – though it is more like toasting – over an open fire. We balance them on hunks of bread and find they are flavoured not just with wood smoke, but with the tang of crushed fern and rowanberries that rises up from the woodland floor. If the crop reappears in following years, this could easily become a local tradition.

NOVEMBER 13 *Burnham Norton, North Norfolk*

Huge flocks of brent geese grazing on the saltmarshes. When they take off the noise is awesome, the rush of wings and urgent morse-code chatter of three thousand birds. It is a solid, almost tangible sound that seems to eddy and crackle through the mass of birds. In flight the flock behaves like a swirling liquid, and birds at the edge have to fly many times faster than those at the centre to keep up with the manoeuvres. Some go in quite the opposite direction to the main body of birds so as to slide into the movement of the vortex.

Wintering brent geese have long been one of Eastern Europe's happiest gifts to us. Almost half of the world's population of the dark-breasted sub-species come to the English east coast from their breeding grounds in the Taymyr Peninsula in Siberia. I saw them arriving in November of 1988, to a Norfolk which was trying to come to terms with the double disaster of dying seals and a polluted North Sea. Each dusk they flew in from the east, along the line of the coast. I was directly underneath them one evening, and found that I involuntarily crouched down. All along the sea wall people were doing the same, kneeling or sitting under the endless dark skeins.

I remembered the tribute which Aldo Leopold wrote just after the last war on the meaning of the geese's return to his Wisconsin farm:

Every March since the Pleistocene, the geese have honked unity from China Sea to Siberian Steppe . . . By this international commerce of geese, the waste corn of Illinois is carried through the clouds to the Arctic tundras, there to combine with the waste sunlight of a nightless June to grow goslings for all the lands between. And in this annual barter of food for light . . . the whole continent receives as net profit a wild poem dropped from the murky skies upon the muds. (*A Sand County Almanack*, 1948)

NOVEMBER 18 *Aldbury, Hertfordshire*

A small male sparrowhawk circles above the lime trees in the grounds of Stocks House. Against the late afternoon sun its wings look almost translucent, as if they are made from lace. No other birds are in the air, but many are hugging low and fearful in the hedges.

NOVEMBER 28 *Suffolk*

A bright but piercingly cold day in High Suffolk. I am meandering around the ancient countryside in the south of the county, a maze of ditches and embankments and ancient boundary trees. Near Groton (from which almost the whole population emigrated in 1630 to found Boston), I pass a road sign warning of 'overhanging eaves'.

Over the Essex border, towards Twinstead, there are ancient copses with the smooth grey poles of small-leaved lime and ancient hedges lining cryptically narrow fields. Towards sunset the wind chills and swings to the north, and as a film of frost begins to form over the fields, hundreds of small birds – chaffinches, fieldfares, tits – begin crowding into whatever shelter they can find in the banks and hedge bottoms. I think of Edward Thomas's poem about hearing an owl on just such a bitter evening in 1915:

> *Speaking for all who lay under the stars*
> *Soldiers and poor, unable to rejoice.*

And, as we drop down the track to our own warm shelter, there, glaring in an oak tree by the house, and seeming no more than a disembodied head in the half-light, is a little owl.

The next day I chance on the isolated church of Tilbury-juxta-Clare, rising like an oasis from the frozen fields. It stands at the end of a rough causeway, a mile from the nearest village, and looking like an ark in this bleak arable landscape. The churchyard is roughly circular in shape, and surrounded by a raised bank of hazel, maple and blackthorn. As is the way with most sites of ancient human settlement, wild and domesticated plants are inextricably jumbled up. In the rough grass, meadow flowers grow next to feral roses, memorial rosemary, and the occasional self-seeded annual from grave-top posies. Here and there are clumps of stinking hellebore (see p. 30) which may be a relic of the time when churchyards doubled as herb gardens. This may also have been the origin of the gladdon iris whose pods of brilliant orange seeds droop under the hedges (the seeds were used as a purgative). But gladdon does occasionally grow wild in shady places here, and was also planted ornamentally, for its

St. Margaret's Church, Tilbury-juxta-Clare, Essex

discreet summer flowers and winter colour.

There is one final link with the old pagan world of plant lore and medicine. High in the lime trees flanking the church entrance are clumps of mistletoe, silhouetted against the setting sun.

FLOWER OF THE MONTH

There is, of course, ivy growing at Tilbury as well, creeping over the older graves and lapping the walls of the church itself.

Aptly, perhaps, ivy blooms at the tail end of the year, from late September through to Christmas. Since the middle of the eighteenth century it has been irrevocably associated with sombre and dark settings, with owls and ruins. Tintern Abbey was the classic site, and the landscape writer, Thomas Whately, graphically described the plant's contribution to the mood of the place in 1770:

> *The shapes of the windows are little altered; but some of them are quite obscured, others partially shaded, by tufts of ivy, and those which are most clear are edged with its slender tendrils, and lighter foliage, wreathing about the sides and the divisions; it winds up the pillars; it clings to the walls; and in one of the aisles, clusters at the top in bunches so thick and so large, as to darken the space below . . . No circumstance so forcibly marks the desolation of a spot once inhabited, as the prevalence of nature over it. (Observations on Modern Gardening, 1770).*

Yet ivy can also be a cheering plant. In early winter its modest green umbels are one of the very few plentiful sources of nectar, and on warm days they can hum with wasps, bees and hoverflies. A couple of months later wood pigeons and thrushes feast off the dark berries.

Ivy is not a parasite, as is still widely believed, but simply uses other trees for support. Sometimes it outlives them and you will find a mop-headed ivy bush just about managing to stand upright on its pliant stems, and looking anything but funereal.

DECEMBER

Great Yarmouth harbour entrance

An off-season seaside holiday – in East Norfolk on this occasion, where the line between new and old views of the sea's edge is very fine.

When Great Yarmouth first became a resort two centuries ago, people came principally for their health, to dose themselves with fashionably therapeutic sea-water and bracing east winds, and the season stretched to all but the coldest months. Now the promenades and piers are like a wind-blown ghost-town for half the year.

But Yarmouth itself doesn't close down. Once the trippers have departed, the town simply turns its back on the beach and, like a migrating salmon, retreats to home base. Old Yarmouth, seafaring rather than seasiding, lies about half a mile inland, clustered around the long harbour that has been formed from the estuaries of the rivers Yare, Bure and Waveney. It has always been a major port, gateway to the Norfolk Broads and once the foremost shipping town in Britain. Up to the late 1960s it was home to a huge herring fleet, and the quay was hectic with packing stations and market stalls. Now the herring is almost fished out and though the town has become a major European container port it hasn't recaptured its old extrovert confidence.

Yarmouth was once just a scattering of huts on a bank of silt and sand which began to form across the Yare-mouth about a thousand years ago. Migratory fishermen from the Kent coast used to camp there during the herring season. The bank, as one contemporary historian put it, 'waxed in height and greatness'. The herring catch waxed mightily, too, and Yarmouth grew into a large and wealthy trading centre. In one of the town's museums there is a beautifully painted topographical map, from 1570, showing the waves of building development following the contours of the slowly receding high-water mark. Another, from two centuries later, notes a population of twelve thousand and shows the unique labyrinth of narrow alleys, known locally as 'rows', which were built at right angles to the river – and to the prevailing wind; only a few survived the terrible damage inflicted on Yarmouth during the Blitz. The Tolhouse museum has one of the slender, one-seat pony carts – 'troll carts' – which were used for transport down them.

All this happened round the harbour. The seafront was ignored until the fashion for seaside holidaying began about 1750. Within thirty years the first theatres and bowling greens had arrived, as well as a pastiche of the troll carts in the form of a lightweight carriage, drawn by two men, in which holidaying ladies were ferried between the entertainment high-spots and the town. One of the earliest commercial souvenirs has also found its way into the Tolhouse collection, a tiny bag of the stuff that made Great Yarmouth famous, with a label reading:

From Yarmouth, where the silv'ry sands
Stretch as far as eye can reach,
Accept this little book of views
And SAMPLE OF THE BEACH

Yarmouth's sands are still a marvel, and at this time of the year you will have them almost to yourself. But you can also explore the larger area of sand and marshland from which, so to speak, Yarmouth was deposited. The odd thing about the landward side of the town is that it has a beach of a kind, too, an area of jumbled paddocks and allotment shacks before the creeks and waterscapes of the flood-plain begin.

Breydon Water is virtually a tidal lake, and was formed after the estuary was sealed off by the sand-bar. It is surrounded by Halvergate Marshes, an immense expanse of grazing marsh claimed out of the swamp by centuries of drainage. But it is still a paradise for wetland birds, especially at this time of year. Scandinavian fieldfares clack from meadow to dyke-side scrub. Flocks of golden plover flash in the distance. Herons flap heavily past the derelict windmills that were once part of the drainage pumping system. Most of these birds fly to Breydon Water to roost and, in late afternoon, the low-tide mud is a vista of tens of thousands of gulls, dunlin and clamouring redshank. Over the sea wall a steady stream of lapwing and curlew fly in from their daytime feeding grounds on the nearby fields.

You can walk to and from the marshes in an afternoon. But on cold evenings you will find the air of melancholy that pervades the seafront has seeped into the town centre. The mist comes down early, the streets drain of people, and seamen and oilrig crews drink introspectively in the corners

137

of pubs. Down by the quay, past the food-packing factories and container bays, is the harbour mouth, cluttered with torn nets and bleached driftwood, and one of the last traces of old Yarmouth.

The harbour entrance is marked by a long line of wooden stanchions, and purple sandpipers bustle for food among the seaweed that coats them. In the distance, against the distant sparkle of the oil-drilling platforms and the glow of the arcades in the town, two columns of pale green lamps mark the entrance to the harbour. One evening I saw a fishing boat coming briskly up the channel, flying three black flags. Not even the Maritime Museum could tell me what this meant, but it felt like a sign of mourning for the lost 'silver harvest' that was once the reason for Yarmouth's existence.

DECEMBER 6 *Stiperstones, Shropshire*

A winter holly wood. Huge, gnarled holly stools amongst a gaunt, rock-strewn landscape.

Holly used to be regularly cut for winter fodder, for sheep and deer. The lopping was done, if possible, relatively high up in the tree, and, over the years, this practice produced a kind of holly pollard. Groups of such trees are often known as 'hollins' and they are scattered about Britain, especially in areas of common grazing land. But few are as ancient and evocative as the squat trees of the Stiperstones.

Other groups survive in the Olchon Valley in Herefordshire and Needwood Forest in Staffordshire. There is a strange (and declining) hollins on pure shingle at Dungeness, Kent (on Holmstone – that is Holly-stone – Beach) that was documented as early as the eighth century.

All holly woods are strange places, and, in geographical terms, are a British speciality. In the New Forest, Hampshire, holly grows in clumps known as 'hats' or 'holms', which provide natural protection for self-seeded oaks and beeches. In Staverton Park and Thicks in Suffolk there are giant hollies amongst the oaks, some actually rooted high up in the forks of the pollard oaks, a two-storey wood.

DECEMBER 15 *Winter train-riding on the Euston line*

Just before it reaches Euston station, the Birmingham line passes through a series of dark chasms in the monumental Victorian brickwork. The sheer soot-stained walls and angled bridge-work almost cut out views of the world beyond, but have been invaded by irrepressible throngs of wild things. Virginia creeper scales the dark tunnel approaches. Pigeons roost on girders. Butterfly bushes sprout out of the tiniest cracks in the stonework. Even at this dead season of the year some dark corners of the stonework are adorned by tufts of bright green ferns, whose spores have ridden in on the slipstream from remote rural woods and found the damp and shade much to their liking.

DECEMBER 18 *Bedfordshire*

An isolated warm day. Wallabies, from down under, basking in the sun on the south-facing slopes of Whipsnade Zoo, enjoying this brief December summer.

DECEMBER 21 WINTER SOLSTICE *Trafalgar Square*

The starling flocks winging in to roost in the West End are

one of the great spectacles of a London winter. Small groups set out from their feeding grounds in the suburbs and mass into larger swarms as they approach the centre. For an hour or so before dark they swirl excitedly round the illuminated theatres and office blocks like a vast black cloak, settling briefly on one building then another.

Just before Christmas, Trafalgar Square is one of the best places to watch them. In the early evenings there is carol singing round the Square's Christmas tree, and, as the songs ring out, the starlings begin to settle down for the night, huddling up for warmth by the shop-front fairy-lights and neon lettering, with just a token personal space between them – proof, on these shortest of days, of the common bonds that link all creatures against the cold.

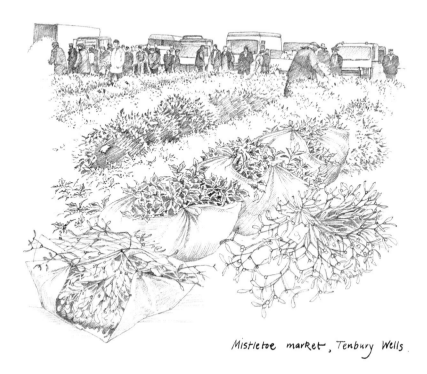

Mistletoe market, Tenbury Wells

LATE DECEMBER *Tenbury Wells, Worcestershire*

The annual mistletoe auction. The market square is full of parcels of mistletoe and holly, and thronging with slight, dark, sideburned smallholders and gipsies from the Welsh border country. Most of the mistletoe is a secondary 'catch' crop from the local orchards, but the holly is a perk from the hedgerows, for landowners and gleaners alike.

The bidding is brisk and high prices are reached. The bundles, bearing hand-written labels from small villages like Berrington and Luston, are loaded onto lorries bound for the wholesale greengrocers in Birmingham.

FLOWER OF THE MONTH

Mistletoe is not usually out in bloom until January, and even then the flowers are a barely conspicuous green tuft. But it is in berry and leaf from November, and is the brightest spot of greenery in the darkest month.

It has been revered since antiquity for its strange presence, rooted high above the ground, shining white and yellow when most other plants are bare, and exploiting its host trees for minerals. In the days of sympathetic magic it was believed to be the master parasite, and therefore capable of overcoming lesser growths and 'excrescences' in humans. The milky berries, held in pairs between the splayed leaves, also suggested its use as an aphrodisiac and fertility potion. The whole plant was considered to be a symbol of new life and spontaneous generation. It would guarantee the crop of the fruit trees in which it grew and, worn round the neck, would ensure peace, divine treasure, open locks . . .

141

In the Welsh borders, the heart of mistletoe country, echoes of these beliefs persisted until early this century. Mistletoe has a natural south-westerly distribution in Britain, but its frequency in this region has a lot to do with the numbers of orchards here. Being planted by birds wiping their beaks after feeding on the berries, mistletoe is common on rough-barked fruit trees. One survey found that it occurred on more than a third of all the apple trees in Herefordshire, and it may have been the constancy of this relationship that kept some of the old fertility rites alive.

In Herefordshire, for instance, mistletoe was bought into cottages and farmhouses on New Year's Eve, and allowed to hang there for the rest of the year, to ensure good luck and a good crop. On some farms the boughs were bound up with hawthorn branches on New Year's morning, set on fire and dragged round the perimeters of the orchard. Eventually (and much influenced by the eighteenth-century fad for Druidism) these local fertility rites became sanitised into the custom of the Christmas kiss; and the Hereford and Worcester fruit-growers came to look on their mistletoe more mundanely, as a useful secondary crop.

Flight of starlings.

EPILOGUE

But the end of the year is not the close of the story. Changes in climate, landscapes and human interests mean that a natural calendar is never fixed or finished. Recently, for example, concern over the loss of traditional orchards has led to the inauguration of 'Apple Day', October 21, for the celebration of fruit in all its vanishing varieties.

The greatest challenge is likely to come from global warming, which may have a profound effect on seasonal landmarks, such as the arrival dates of summer birds and the flowering times of woodland plants. Bluebells may become scarcer in southern Britain, continental birds like the hoopoe become regular breeders, the East Anglian marshes advance many more miles inland. How well we cope with these changes will depend in part on whether we can learn from the natural world's resilient and inventive responses to the vagaries of the seasons – some of which I hope I have given a glimpse of in this book.

INDEX

(*Page numbers in italic refer to illustrations*)

Abernethy Forest
43
Aldbury 130
Alder buckthorns
60
alders 19, 40, 122
algae, blue-green
112
Allsop, Kenneth 29,
90–1
Ambleside 75
anemones 23
Anemone blanda
47
wood 22
angelica, wild 107
ants
flying 102–3
red 102
aphids 107
Apple Day 143
apple trees 142
apples
Bramley 26
crab 119
wilding 119
ashes (trees) 13, 19,
37, 108, 125

Ashridge Park 120
aspens 19, 70
Auden, W. H. 67,
69
Aust 12
avocets 74
Avonmouth 13
Awre 12
Aylesbury, Vale of
34–5
azaleas, wild 99

bank and ditch
boundaries 21
Barking, Suffolk 45
Barnham Cross
Common 82
Bath 125
bats
Natterer's 30
noctule 114
beans
broad 81
mung 107
Beaulieu, River 60
Bedfordshire 139
beech tufts 120

beeches 20, 22, 37,
53, 54, 60, 120,
139
mast 90
bees 59, 134
beetles 22, 59, 100
pollen 61
Beinn Eighe 99
Belgrave Square,
London 106,
117
Belgravia 106
Berkeley nuclear
power station
89
Berrington 141
birches 19
bistort, Alpine 81
bittercress, hairy *15*
bitterns 46
blackberries 100,
119
blackbirds 24–5,
26, 27, 30, 43,
56, 128
blackcaps 42
Blackdown Hills
36–40, 41

blackthorns 45, 47, 57, 59, 73, 131
Blakeney Point 92
Bloomsbury 95
bluebells 44, 53, 143
Blythe, Ronald 114
Bodleian Library, Oxford 94
Bodmin Moor 40
Bolderwood 114
Botanic Garden, Oxford 94–5
Bourne (stream) 32–3
boxwoods 124
bracken 100
Bradgate 20
Brandon 82, 83
Breckland 57, 73, 79, 82–6
Breydon Water 137
briars, wild 76
brimstone butterflies 44, 45
Broad Street Station 109
Brooke, Humphrey 77
broom 62
prostrate 58
Buckingham Palace Gardens 116
Buckinghamshire 49, 91, 98
buddleias 80, 91, 104, 110, *110* see also butterfly bushes
bullaces 119
bullfinches 108
bulrushes 122

bumblebees 59
Bunyard, Edward 118
Bure, River 136
burnet great 75
salad 71
Burnham Beeches 20
Burnham Deepdale 46
Burnham Market 8
Burnham Norton 46, 74, 129
Burren 71
Bury St Edmunds 84
bustards, great 85
buttercups 67
butterflies 21, 44, 45, 79, 80, 91, 101, 103, 104
butterfly bushes (*Buddleia davidii*) 139
buzzards 57, 63

calves 72
Cambridgeshire 34, 49
Camden 95, 108
Camden Town Group 38
campion 55
sea 62
capercaillies 43
carrots 85
caterpillars 61, 92
cats 95
cattle 12, 20
celandines 27
ceps 118–19
chaffinches 25, 131

cherries (trees) 45, 47, 61, 124
wild 128
cherries, wild 88
chert-stone 36, 38
Cherwell, River 22
Cheshire 35, 97
Chess Valley 53, 91, 100, 103
chestnuts, sweet 118
chestnuts (trees) 81, 100
chiffchaffs 2
Chilterns 9, 20, 33, 35–6, 47, 53, 54, 63, 71, 91, 100, 103, 120, 124, 128
choughs 62
cinquefoil 81
Clare, County 71
Clayhidon 38
clouded yellow butterflies 79, 80
Colchicum autumnale 125–6
comma butterflies 45
conifers 37, 73
coots 122
coppicing *18*, 19–20, 21, 22, 50, 57, 93
coralroot 53
coriander 117
corn 33, 71
corn buntings 25, 26, 44
corncrakes 71
Cornwall 22, 29, 40–1, 47, 51–2

Cotswolds 22
Covent Garden 95
cow parsley 54, 60
cowberries 99
cowslips 45, 49, 51, 70
cranesbills
  bloody 70, 74
  wild 67
Cressbrook Dale 70
Crete 78
Crippen, Dr Hawley 116
crocuses, saffron 125
crows 63, 106
  carrion 25–6, 74
cuckoo flowers 53, 55
cuckoos 53, 71
Culm, River 38
Cumbria 75
cumin 117
curlews 43–4, 62, 75, 137
currants 44
cypresses, swamp 95

daffodils, wild (Lent lilies) 38, *39*, 41, 47
daisies 15
  Galinsoga parviflora (Gallant Soldiers) 117
  michaelmas 81, 109, 116
  ox-eye 62
damsons 119
dandelions 15
deadly nightshade 23

Dean, Forest of 12, 20, 89
deer 20
  roe 43
Dentdale 67
Derbyshire 70
  Dales 93
Devon 41
dewberries 119
dippers 67
divers,
  black-throated 43
Dockland, London 109
Doddershall Wood 53
dogwoods 124
Dommett 37
dormice 21, 30
Dorset 29, 57, 86
Doubleday, Henry (botanist) 49
doves, turtle 71
Dowrog Common 62
dragonflies 95, 100
  emperor 109
ducks 122
  mallards 22
Dungeness 57–9, 138
Dunkeswell 38
dunlins 12, 14, 104, 137
Durham, County 81
Dyfed 57
Dymock *39*, 41

East Anglia 7, 12, 29, 41, 49, 50, 73, 83, 84, 93, 143

see also Norfolk; Suffolk
Egton Bridge 97
elders 59
  dwarf 109
  flowers 81
Ellesborough 124
elms 35–6, 41
Elveden 85
elvers 12
Emily's Wood 85
Epping 20
Essex 22, 49, 49–50
Evelyn, John 82
Exmoor 36, 37

Fal, River 40–1
falcons 99–100, 127
  hobby 91, 112–13
  kestrels 100, 108, 127
Farndale 41
Farrer, Reginald 64
Fenland 73
fennel 117
fern-owls *see* nightjars
ferns 55, 117, 129, 139
fieldfares 26, 33, 127, 131, 137
flags, sweet 107
flint 83, 84
flycatchers 56
  spotted 90–1
Forestry Commission 84, 85, 86
Fountains Fell 67
foxes 71, 107

Framilode 89
Frampton 12
fritillaries, snake's
    head 47
frogs 30
frosts 27
fungi 120
Furness 20

Galinsoga parviflora
    see daisies
garlic 55
geese 14
    brent *127*,
    129–30
    Canada 108
Gerard, John 41,
    125
germander
    speedwell 55
Gibson, George
    (botanist) 49
Gloucestershire 20,
    27, 41, 49
gnats 11, 128
goats 72
golden rod,
    American 116
goldfinches 25
gooseberries 88,
    95–7
Goostrey 97
gorse 62, 63, 82,
    114
goshawks 45, 85
gram 117
Grand Union Canal
    107
Grasmere 41
grass, canary 117
grasshoppers 100
Grassington 67

Great Bardfield
    49–50
Great Yarmouth
    135–8
    harbour entrance
    135
grebes 122
    great crested 106
greenfinches 23,
    111
Grendon Woods
    53
Grigson, Geoffrey,
    *A Herbal Of
    All Sorts*
    47–9
Grimes Graves 83
Groton 130
groundsel 14
gulls 137
    black-headed 25

Hackney 105
    Cut 109
    Marsh 108
hailstorm 70
Halvergate Marshes
    137
Hampshire 22, 41,
    57, 60, 93, 100,
    138
Hardings Wood 3,
    128
Hardraw Force 68
Hardy, Thomas 86
harebells 102
harriers 57, 74
    marsh 44, 103
Harrow 44
Hawes 68
Hawkley 33
haws 119

hawthorns 60, 108,
    127
hazels 37, 38, 60,
    70, 131
    nuts 118
heath, heather 62,
    82
hedges 21, 84, 131
hellebore 31
    stinking
    (*Helleborus
    foetidus*) 30,
    131
Hemel Hempstead
    54, 80
hemlock 30
Hemyock 37
hen-harriers 8
henbane 116
herb Paris 55
herbs 23
Herefordshire 20,
    49, 138, 142
herons 33, 108,
    122, 127, 137
herrings 136
Hertfordshire 31,
    49, 55, 79, 112,
    130
Hickling Broad 103
High Wycombe 20
Highlands, Western
    99
hogweed 15
    giant 116
Holkham 8
hollies 138–9
    prostrate 59
hollins 138
Hollow Lanes,
    Selborne 55–6
Holmstone 59
    Beach 138

honey fungus 28
hoopoes 143
hops, wild 111, 122
hoverflies 134
Hyde Park 106, 107

Icknield Way 83,
    85–6
Ingleborough 69
    Hill 66–7
insects 30, 45, 55,
    56, 58–9, 61–2,
    100, 119
irises 44, 81
    gladdon 24, 131
ivy 133–4

jackdaws 69
Jefferies, Richard,
    *Wild Life in a
    Southern County*
    128
junipers 19
    prostrate 74

Kent 57–9, 138
kestrels 100, 108,
    127
Kew Gardens 117
kidney vetch 62
kingfishers 10
King's Forest 86
kites, red 57
Knossos 78
knots (birds) 14,
    104

Ladbroke Grove
    107

Lake District 22, 93
Lakenheath 57
    Warren 82, 83
Lamorran Wood 40
Lancashire 20, 74
Langstrothdale 67
lapwings 53, 75,
    137
lavants
    (winterbournes)
    33
lavender 25
Lea Bridge 108
Leicestershire 20
Leigh 38
Lent lilies *see*
    daffodils, wild
Leopold, Aldo, *A
    Sand County
    Almanack* 130
lichens 22, 41, 59
    stagshorn 58
lilac 43, 44, 99
lilies 22
    of the valley 68,
    70
Limes (trees) 22,
    130
    blossom 92–3, *93*
    large-leaved 93
    small-leaved (*Tilia
    cordata*) 17, 93,
    130–1
    Tilia x vulgaris
    92–3
limestone 64, 66–9,
    70, 93
Lincolnshire 22, 93
lindens *see* limes
Little Venice 107
Littondale 67
lobelias 117
Loch Garten 43

London 54, 95,
    105–11,
    115–17,
    139–40
London Pride 115
loosestrife, purple
    108
lungworts 60
Luston 141

Magdalen Meadows,
    Oxford 22, 47,
    48, 98
magnolias 95
maidens (tree
    forms) 21
Malham 67
mallards 22
maples 56, 60, 124,
    131
    field 128
marjoram 102
martins 45, 46, 74,
    100, 103
    house 3, 46, 53,
    53, 54, 60–1,
    63–4, 74–5,
    87–91 *passim,
    94*, 96, 101–2,
    106, 108–13
    passim, 121–2,
    124, 128
Marton 97
May blossom 54,
    60
mayflies 62
meadowsweet 89
*Megalithes aeneas
    see* moths,
    longhorn
Mendips 125, 126
Mens 20

merlins 127
mice 28
Millais, Sir John
    Everett 108
millet 107
mistletoe 23, 49,
    93, 133, 141–2
    auction *140*, 141
    pear-tree 13
Moccas 20
moles 30
moneywort 47
moon 56
    eclipse of 23–4
moorhens 107, 127
Morris dancing 2
mosses 22, 58
moths 59, 99
    longhorn (*Mega-
    lithes aeneas*) 61
    puss 92
Moughton Fell 69
mushrooms
    ceps 118–19
    field 118–19
    oyster 120
    parasol 118–19,
    128–9
myrtle, bog 114

Needwood Forest 138
New Forest 20, 22,
    60, 73, 114, 138
nightingales 56–7,
    73
nightjars
    (fern-owls)
    71–3, 84, 85
nightshade, deadly
    116
Norfolk 2, 49, 73,
    82–6, 103

Broads 122–3,
    123, 136
    East 135
    North 3, 7, 7–8,
    23–4, 46, 74,
    92, 129
North Creake 24
Northampton 125
Nottingham
    catchfly 58
nuthatches 25, 26

oaks 19, 22, 40, 41,
    139
'Obby 'Oss
    ceremony
    51–2
oil-seed rape 61
Olchon Valley 138
old man's beard 15,
    128
orchids 22, 71
    bee 91–2
    marsh 81, 86–7
    purple 22, 55, 70
orioles, golden 73
orpines 60
ospreys 43
Otter, River 38–40
otters 40
Ouse Washes 34
owls 28–30, 113,
    131
    barn 28–30
    little 131
    short-eared 8, 13
Oxford 2, 3, *16*,
    22–3, 47, 94–5
Oxfordshire 52–3
oxlips 31, *42*, 49–50
oystercatchers 7,
    62, 68

Padstow 51–2
pansies 81
pastures 41
peanut bushes 117
peat-mines 122–3
Peddars Way 86
Pembrokeshire 62
pennywort, wall 38
Peover 97
peregrines 62, 63,
    69, 99–100
Petrie, Sir Flinders
    77
pheasants 50, 84,
    105
philadelphus 95
pigeons 9–10, 50,
    69, 106, 107,
    139
    wood 43, 134
pines 84, 85, 95
Pitstone Fen 91
plover
    golden 137
    ringed 104
plums, wild 119
Plynlimon 27
pollarding 13, 20,
    21, 34, 93, *98*,
    138, 139
Poplar 109
poplars, black 31,
    31, 34–5, 45
poppies 71, 81, 117
primroses 15, 41,
    44, 45, 47, 49,
    80
    bird's-eye 49, 64,
    65, 66, 69
Primula elatior
    49–50
purple emperor 21
purslane 92

pussy willows 23

quails 71
Quantocks 36, 37
quartz 99

rabbits 83
ragwort 23
  London 115
  Oxford *16*
railways 79–81,
  139
rampion 102
Ranworth 122
raspberries 88, 119
rats 28
rattle, red 64
ravens 63
red admiral 103
redcurrants 88
redshanks 68, 137
redstarts, black 109,
  111
redwings 8, 33, 127
reeds 122
Regent's Park,
  London 108,
  116
Richmond 117
ring ouzels 46
robins 43, 99
rock-roses 66
  hoary 74
rocket, London 115
Romney Marsh 57
rooks 53
rose-bay willow
  herb 115
rosemary 131
roses 2, 76–8

'Abyssinian' (*Rosa
  richardii*) 77–8,
  77
burnet (*Rosa
  pimpinellifolia*)
  70, 76
dog (*Rosa canina*)
  76
downy (*Rosa
  tomentosa*) 76
'Dunwich' 76
field (*Rosa
  arvensis*) 76
guelder 122
'Holy' *see* roses,
  'Abyssinian'
'Omar Khayyam'
  77
Rosa villosa 76
sweet briar (*Rosa
  eglanteria*) 76
wild 131
'Wolley-Dod's' 76
'Woolverstone
  Church' 77
Ross and Cromarty 99
rowans 100, 119
  berries 119, 129
Roydon Wood 60
Ruan Lanihorne 40
rue, meadow 74
rushes 64

saffron, meadow
  (*Colchicum
  autumnale*)
  125–6
St Austell 40
St David's Head 62
St Filii de los
  Eglosros 29

St James's Park,
  London 105–7
St Michael Penkevil
  41
salmon 12
saltmarshes *127*
samphire 2, 92
sandpipers 43, 112
  buff-breasted 104
  curlew 104
  purple 138
sandstone 99
Santon Downham
  82, 84
saxifrage 55
  meadow 70
Scandrett Street
  Churchyard,
  London 110
scarecrows 9–10
Scott, Sir Peter 13
sea 58, 92
sea kale 58
sea lavender 92
sea wormwood 92
seals 129
Selborne 30, 33, *51*,
  55–6, 72, 89,
  100
senna, bladder 116
service trees 95
  wild 60, 119–20
serviceberries *118*,
  119–20
Severn, River
  Bore 12
  Estuary 11–14,
  89–90
Shadwell 109–10
Shakespeare,
  William, *The
  Winter's Tale* 49

Shap Fell 64
Sharpness 13
sheep 83
sheep's-bit 62
Shepperton 117
Shepton Mallet 125
shrews, water 30
Shropshire 138
Siberia 129
Simmonds, Posy
113
siskins 23, 25, 26
skullcap 107
Slimbridge 13–14
sloes 119
snowberries 24, 47
snowdrops 22
Solomon's seal 55
Somerset 36–40
sorrel, wood 22
South Downs Way
102
South Walsham
122
sparrowhawks 9,
45, 100, 112,
127, 130
sparrows 25, 75, 89,
106, 108, 122
spiders 34, 101
crab 86–7
money 115
spindles (trees) 124
spurge laurels 15,
60
squill, spring 62
squirrels 118
red 43
Staffordshire 138
Staple Fitzpaine 36
starlings 25, 26,
111, 112,
139–40, 142

Staverton Park 139
Stiffkey 92
Stiperstones 138
Stocks House 130
stonechats 63
stools (tree forms)
20–1
Stratford Marsh 109
strawberries 88
wild 66, 74
stubs (trees) 21
Studland Heath 86
Suffolk 7, 18, 22,
44, 45, 49, 50,
57, 71, 73, 76,
77, 104, 130,
139
sundews 75
Sussex 20, 41, 57,
102
Swaffham 84, 85
swallows 2, 30, 46,
72, 74, 81, 89,
100, 113
swans 34
Bewick's 8, 14
whooper 43
sweet corn 107
Swettenham 97
swifts 2, 45, 52, 54,
55, 81, 87,
111–12
sycamores 44, 51

Taunton, Vale of 36
Taymyr Peninsula
129
teal 11
Teign Valley 41
Tenbury Wells 140,
141
terns 46, 58

Thames, River 109
Thaxted 49
Thetford 23–4
Thicks 139
Thomas, Edward
131
The Heart of
England 94–5
thornapples 116
thrift 62
thrushes 26, 56,
134
mistle 24, 26, 43
winter 128
thyme 71, 102
wild 67
Tilbury-juxta-Clare
131, 132
Tintern Abbey 133
tits 25, 131
blue 122
long-tailed 34,
111
toadstools 81, 125,
128
Tolhouse museum,
Great
Yarmouth
136–7
tomatoes 107, 117
tortoises 121
Trafalgar Square
139–40
Traherne, Thomas
102
Tregony 40
Tring Reservoirs 55,
112
Truro 41
tumbleweed, prairie
116–17
Turner, J. M. W. 68
Turner, William 125

turnips 84
Twinstead 130
Tyneham 57

Underbarrow Scar
74
Upottery 38–40
Upper Greensand
36
Upper Teesdale 81

viburnums 95
vines, Russian 109
Virginia creeper 89,
139
voles 103

wagtails 11, 112
grey 109, 127
pied 128
yellow 74
Walberswick 44,
73, 104
Wales 19, 27, 57,
142
wallabies 139
Walthamstow 108
Wangford Warren
85

warblers 56
Dartford 114–15
reed 74
willow 43
wood 44
wasps 134
waterfalls 68
watermelons 117
Watford 54, 81
Waveney, River
136
Weald 20, 102
weasels 30
Weathercote 68
Wembley 80, 81
wheat 107
whetstone, banded
69
Whipsnade Zoo 139
white admiral 21
White, Gilbert 29,
30, 33, 72, 73,
89, 128
whitebeams 119
whitefronts 8
whitethroats 71, 81
wigeon 11, 34
Wigginton 3
Wildfowl Trust,
Slimbridge
13–14
willows 40, 44, 111

pollard 98
weeping 95
winterbournes
32–3, 45
Wisconsin 130
wood-pasture 20
woodlands 16–22,
60, 82–3, 100
coppiced 18
tidal 40–1
woodlarks 85
woodpeckers 75
woodruffs 60
sweet 22, 55
Worcestershire 20
woundwort, marsh
107
Wye, River 20
Valley 21, 93
Wyre Forest 20,
125

Yare, River 136
yellowhammers 26,
30
yews 68
Yorkshire 49, 64,
65, 97
Dales 19, 46,
66–9
Young, Arthur 83